About

The author is a retired doctor. His father, two uncles (one was once an assistant in a practice in Hawick) and a cousin, were also doctors.

He was married to his wife June (also a doctor) for over fifty years (her great uncle was once a GP in Hawick).

Of his four children, two are doctors. Three of his grandchildren have also followed down the medical path.

MEMOIRS OF A COUNTRY DOCTOR

Peter Paterson-Brown

MEMOIRS OF A COUNTRY DOCTOR

Vanguard Press

VANGUARD PAPERBACK

© Copyright 2020
Peter Paterson-Brown

The right of Peter Paterson-Brown to be identified as author
of
this work has been asserted by him in accordance with the
Copyright, Designs and Patents Act 1988.

A CIP catalogue record for this title is
available from the British Library.

ISBN 978 1 78465 763 5

*Vanguard Press is an imprint of
Pegasus Elliot MacKenzie Publishers Ltd.*
www.pegasuspublishers.com

First printed in 2018
Reprinted twice in 2019

First Published in 2020

**Vanguard Press
Sheraton House Castle Park
Cambridge England**

Printed & Bound in Great Britain

Dedication

To June who gave me my family and to my patients who gave me their trust and friendship.

FOREWORD

During my forty years as a doctor, two were spent working in various hospitals in Edinburgh, thirty-four as a general practitioner or GP in a practice in the Borders of Scotland, and finally a few years doing locums (temporary work) in three different practices in the Scottish Highlands.

Learning on the job as a newly qualified doctor, unsure of many aspects of my role, meant some problems with communication and I encountered births and deaths and in between found my feet. Patients, young and old, delightful and difficult, and colleagues presented challenges to be met, both medical and otherwise. From a toddler with a mysterious illness, to a young rascal with a hook in his hand from poaching, a philandering colleague and an elderly lady who wanted to rewrite her will, I had to cope with them all – not to mention the arrival of modern technology.

All the stories are based on real events in my life; one when I was a houseman in hospital, and all the rest when I was a GP. The stories, although based on fact, are all altered so that the characters are unrecognisable and if you think it could be you, it isn't, or is it? Likewise, all names and (frequently) places have also been changed.

I say almost all the stories are based on real life events but I must admit the only true part of the last story is the alibi which I witnessed with my own eyes.

Contents

Never had it so good

Long before Harold Macmillan made this remark, and so gave birth to a popular catch phrase, I came across it from a most unexpected source. To put you in the picture let me take you back to the summer of 1956. I was a houseman in the Royal Infirmary (in Edinburgh, of course); I say of course because no other Infirmary in the UK is called the Royal. You can't get any lower in the medical pecking order than houseman. My duty as houseman was to clerk in the patients, who were admitted either from the waiting list or from A&E as an emergency, and look after their needs before and after their operation. The wards, unlike today, were the old Florence Nightingale ones which had eight beds down each side of the ward and several down the middle, the exact number depending on the need. The custom was for each ward to admit emergencies on a certain day each week; we admitted all emergencies on a Saturday and would do that for six months. If we had more admissions than beds, we 'put up' the required number of beds down the middle of the ward. Along both sides of the wards, windows stretched from the floor to the ceiling; the views were spectacular; looking south over the Meadows towards the Blackford Hills, or north over the body of Edinburgh.

There was a considerable amount of building going on in those days and, just like today, the skyline was dotted with cranes which seemed to grow taller and taller and their horizontal arms stretching further and further out in an almost predatory way, hovering like an eagle, wings out, waiting to pounce on its prey. I loved those cranes and never understood how they were built, and they had a hypnotic effect on me. They were clearly visible even to patients who were bedridden.

One summer's evening I admitted a Polish man from A&E who had a large inguinal hernia and good control of the English language; this was an unusual combination in those days, but very welcome as I knew a bit about hernias but did not have 'the Polish' as people who spoke Gaelic would say. As the most junior member of the surgical team it was my responsibility to 'clerk him in'. This meant I had to take an extremely detailed history and make an equally detailed examination of him before the consultant saw him at all. The history was extensive and included the following:

1. Present Illness.
2. Past Illnesses.
3. Family History.
4. Social History – Housing e.g. Flat (owned/rented/ground floor/tenth floor), Diet,

Alcohol consumption, Smoking… You name it, we would want to know it.

There really was not much I didn't know about the patient by the time I had finished taking his history, and you can bet your bottom dollar that, if there was, the consultant would spot it and that would mean trouble for me.

Having taken his history, I was about to embark on my examination, and it had to be equally thorough or there would be more trouble for me. However, let me just tell you a little about Mr Drosky. He was middle aged which in 1956 was fifty or even late forties. He had been born in Poland but left with his parents before war broke out. He fled first to France and then on to England, then spent most of the war in Scotland staying with a distant relative on his mother's side. Mr Drosky worked on a farm and after the war joined an agricultural company that sold all manner of farm machinery. His knowledge and charming personality resulted in his fairly rapid promotion, and in time he became a senior salesman and travelled extensively in Europe. Sadly he developed, probably because of a tendency to asthma as a child, chronic bronchitis as an adult and this accounted for many visits to various hospitals in his native Poland, France, Germany, Bulgaria and of course the UK.

"I could tell you a thing or two about some of the hospitals I've been in, Doctor," Mr Drosky said with a smile.

"Yes, Mr Drosky, I'm sure you could but not just now, I really must make progress and complete my examination of you."

"Maybe tomorrow then, Doctor, provided I survive the operation." He laughed. "Only joking, Doctor. Will you be doing it?"

"Good heavens no. Fortunately for your sake one of my seniors will; they are all very good. Now, let me take your pulse; lie back and relax."

He did as I requested and settled himself comfortably. I took a firm grip of his wrist and felt his radial pulse. "Please don't speak whilst I'm counting; I do need to concentrate." Slowly I began to count, not out aloud but just to myself. One, two, three, drop beat, four, five... and that was when the purpose of this tale really will become apparent. As I stood holding his pulse and counting, I happened to be glancing out of the window, six, seven, my attention was caught by a quite extraordinary sight. A man had come out of the small cabin on the top of one of the enormous cranes that I mentioned earlier. Now I can't stand heights; even the lower spring board in the local swimming pool was an absolute no-no for me. Fascinated by this man I watched in horror as he began to walk along the horizontal arm that stretched out ahead of him. What on earth was he up to I couldn't imagine; I had never seen anything like it; the further he walked the more alarmed I became. Then suddenly I realised exactly what he was going to do: he was going to jump off the end. He was going to commit suicide; there was no other explanation. Now hearing of a suicide is, especially if the person is known to you, a most upsetting business, but to actually witness it, is a shattering experience. I did not know what to do; I was totally impotent and in an extraordinary way I felt unable to shut my eyes or look away. I felt faint and could feel myself breaking out in a sweat. He reached the end, looked down at his feet, bent forward to do something, then in one sudden movement swivelled round and I could tell he was going to do a backward dive. I was still unable to shut my eyes. I just stared absolutely transfixed. Then he began to walk back along the crane, climbed into the cabin and disappeared from sight. I felt quite sick and shook my head.

"Doctor, is there something wrong with my pulse?" Mr Drosky asked anxiously.

I came rapidly back to earth and realised I had been holding Mr Drosky's wrist for several minutes. "No, it's fine, absolutely fine – very good," I replied, I hope reassuringly.

"Well, Doctor, let me tell you something. I have been in many hospitals as I told you earlier, but never ever have I had such a meticulous examination of my pulse, and I suppose my circulation, that you have just given me, absolutely incredible; no wonder the Royal has such a good reputation."

"Very kind of you to say so. Now let me listen to your chest."

I finished my examination without further excitement. "Excellent, you are in good health. Your chest is fine, and you should have no trouble with the operation. You will be operated on tomorrow morning."

"Thank you, Doctor, meantime I shall just lie back and enjoy the view."

"You do that. I'll see you tomorrow."

That really should be the end of this story, after all it's enough, isn't it? A nice man had been kind enough to give me totally undeserved praise which didn't do any harm and which rarely came my way. But there is a little more to relate. About two weeks later in the *Evening News*, a newspaper that came out every afternoon on the streets of Edinburgh around three or four o'clock, was a letter part of which I must let you read.

'Dear Sir, I recently had the occasion to be a patient in the Royal Infirmary of Edinburgh to have an operation. I have been in many hospitals in Europe but I have never had treatment like I received in the Royal. It was outstanding, and the patience and care I received from the admitting doctor was quite remarkable; no wonder the hospital is called the '*Royal* Infirmary'.

I must remember in the swings and roundabouts of life that there are times when you get unfairly criticised, but there are also times when you get undeserved praise.

The doctor who didn't know

After my honeymoon in 1957 I had a free month before
I took up a post as an SHO (Senior House Officer, one
rung up the ladder from Houseman), in the Sick
Children's Hospital in Edinburgh, so I decided to apply
for a fortnight's locum which had been advertised in the
BMJ (British Medical Journal). It was in a small mining
town a few miles north of Stirling. I had never worked
other than in a hospital and had always had all my work
supervised. I was not allowed to admit or discharge a
patient without a consultant or senior registrar (almost a
consultant) checking that my request was correct. I felt
it was time I found out what 'Life' was like in the wider
world; after all I was pretty sure I knew an awful lot of
medicine; well I had done six years as a student! I
thought a fortnight in General Practice would be
interesting, not very demanding and I could do with the
money (a houseman in 1956 was paid only £23 a
month). I received a phone call a couple of days after I
had posted my application, from a Doctor Norman, who
informed me that he would like me to start on Monday
the first of April; maybe I should have considered that a
bad omen, but I didn't. I was asked to come for lunch on
the Sunday and Doctor Norman then planned to show

me round the practice and he would depart on the Monday for Majorca.

He lived in a house which had belonged to his predecessor. It was situated close to a railway level-crossing. Apparently, his predecessor had a habit of visiting the pub which was about a quarter of a mile away, also close to the railway line. It was the doctor's habit to walk home along the railway line and when he reached the level-crossing he knew he was home. It was a single line railway and on one occasion the doctor met a train and that was how Doctor Norman inherited the practice.

Doctor Norman was a friendly soul and it was obvious, when he took me round his practice, that the patients liked him. He was a chain smoker and thought nothing of smoking whilst consulting with or examining a patient: indeed, he was sitting on a patient's bed examining him when the ash fell off his cigarette; nothing daunted he removed his silk hanky from his breast pocket and dusted the ash from the patient's tummy. He finished his tour of the practice by showing me his surgery. Well it wasn't just his surgery, apparently he shared it with two other doctors who were in different practices. It really was a glorified hut and it was pretty basic.

"You will consult here from nine a.m. till eleven a.m. and five p.m. till six p.m. It is very important you don't exceed these times as the other doctors will arrive expecting to start their surgeries. If you haven't seen all the patients they will just leave and come back in the evening, if they feel it's worthwhile. Most of them will only be wanting a medical certificate for their work. The system is very simple: if they work seven shifts a week down the mine, they get paid for eight but if they only work six shifts they will require a medical certificate to cover the seventh and that will then count as eight shifts! It is very important that you charge half a crown for each certificate. There is a labelled jar in the desk drawer and here is the key to it and here is the surgery key and my house key. One other thing, have you had a lot of experience prescribing?"

"Well not a lot, no." Actually, I had none.

"No problem, most of the patients come complaining of a cough as you would expect and even if they don't, ask them if they have a cough and you can give them a note saying either red or yellow bottle please, and the chemist will give them the appropriate medicine. The red is best for a night cough and the yellow best for a day cough. It may sound a bit strange to you but most of the patients are hardy souls and really all they want is that certificate. Any questions?"

"No, I don't think so," I replied feeling slightly confused.

"Oh, one other thing, you have to go to the dentist in Stirling on Tuesday afternoon at two p.m. to give a few gases. Done much anaesthetics?"

"No," I replied rather anxiously. It didn't seem to bother Doctor Norman, but it sure bothered me.

And so Monday saw my initiation into general practice. My first patient, a John Grieve, didn't beat about the bush. "Morning, Doctor, just come for my certificate; here's the half crown."

"Good morning," Mr Grieve. "What's the problem?"

"No problem, Doctor, not now, but had diarrhoea on Saturday so couldn't do my shift."

"Do you have diarrhoea often?"

"Now and then."

"Any blood in your stools?" I remembered this was an important question.

"In my what?"

"Your stools, your motions. Your bowel motions. Any blood in them?"

"I don't know I've never looked," he replied, rather perplexed.

"I think you had better pop up on the couch and I will examine you."

"Oh no, that's not necessary. Doctor Norman knows all about my health. I just need the certificate." Reluctantly I wrote one out and swapped it for half a crown. It didn't seem a very good way to practice, I thought. After all I hadn't taken a proper history, hadn't examined him; he might have a carcinoma of his bowel. I made a note to tell Doctor Norman about John Grieve when he came home. I got up and went to the waiting room, which was alarmingly full.

"Next please." A very large man stood up and followed me into the surgery. "Morning," I said, "do sit down."

"Thank you, Doctor. I need a certificate. I couldn't work on Saturday; my migraines were terrible."

"Have you had them long?"

"Off and on for a year or two."

I got up and pulled the curtain shut. "Right, let's have a look at your eyes." I took out my new ophthalmoscope and said, "Look up at the picture over there please." I looked in both his eyes, they seemed fine to me. "Do you get sick when you get these migraines?"

"No, Doctor, not unless I've had a skin-full." He laid a half crown on my desk and somewhat pathetically I gave him a certificate stating: *This patient says he had a migraine on Saturday and couldn't work.*

Dr Norman was right, almost all the patients wanted a certificate or occasionally a prescription for a cough bottle. It took quite a while to examine the chest as I had been taught and by eleven o'clock I had only seen half the waiting room. How Doctor Norman got through so many patients in the allotted time I had no idea. This was certainly a steep learning curve. I passed the incoming doctor on my way out and he merely nodded at me. "You're running late," he said in a rather unfriendly tone.

I looked at my watch, it was only a quarter past eleven. I stopped at the reception desk. "Sorry, I'm afraid I couldn't see them all. Is it normally so busy?"

"No, but there was a football match on Saturday and the miners do like their football, so that always causes a lot of certificates to be required on the Monday to cover the missed shift. The ones you haven't managed to see this morning will be back tonight. Would you like me to print out a batch of certificates and then all you need to do is sign them?"

"Well that's very kind of you but you won't know what diagnosis to put on them, will you?"

"No problem, Doctor, I'll just put *This patient was incapacitated due to illness.*"

"And will that be sufficient?" I asked, slightly surprised.

"Oh yes. That's what we do for Doctor Norman."

"Well, thank you. You are most helpful." And shaking my head, departed the surgery.

The evening surgery went very well and I was home in time for supper.

"How did your day go?" my wife, June, asked.

"Well once I got the hang of it, not badly. It's a bit different to hospital medicine. No time for taking a history or examining the patient, so actually it's pretty easy. Tomorrow could be more difficult as I have to give some anaesthetics for a dentist in Stirling."

"But do you know how to?" she asked.

"No, not really. Remember we only gave six in our final year and to be honest it was the consultant who gave them and we just held the mask. Did you do more?" (June had been a student in the same year.)

"No, you'd better be careful."

Tuesday came and with it trouble in more ways than I expected. The dentist asked me if I was experienced and I said no. "Well the good news is I've only two cases and they should be quite straight forward. Just make them anoxic and I'll be as quick as I can." (Anoxic means deprived of oxygen.)

The first case was a five-year-old girl. I turned the machine on full and was amazed at how quickly she became blue and unconscious. He removed the tooth in a flash, but it then took about twenty minutes for the girl to come round. I think I had given her too much gas! The next case was a teenage boy who proved incredibly strong, and I had great difficulty holding him down and at the same time administering the gas.

Half the time the mask slid off his face and I breathed as much gas as he did; it was touch and go whether he or I became unconscious first. When I came round, it was a bit embarrassing to find the dentist and the teenager chatting whilst I was lying on the floor.

"Thank you, Doctor, that's all for today."

"What about next Tuesday?" I said rather anxiously.

"No, I've nothing scheduled for then," he replied quickly.

The rest of the day passed without any problem. The evening surgery was surprisingly quiet; I wondered if word had got round that Doctor Norman was on holiday. It was close on nine o'clock when the phone rang. "Doctor, could you come and see Jamie? He's not well; he's very feverish."

"Yes, what's the address?"

"Thirty-seven Queens Place."

"I'll be round shortly."

I looked up the map Doctor Norman had left for me and set off. Queens Place was a long road of miners' terraced houses, all identical and all painted with the same dull brown paint and the same grey front door. Number thirty-seven was about halfway along. There were no cars nearby and I parked outside and rang the bell. A young man opened the door. "What do you want?" he said rather abruptly.

"I'm Doctor Neville. Doctor Norman is on holiday."

"Oh sorry, come in. I'm William."

We shook hands and I followed him in to the kitchen/ living room. "This is my wife Mary. This is Doctor Neville, Mary. Doctor Norman is on holiday."

"Thank you, Doctor. It's Jamie. He's not right at all."

"How old is Jamie, Mary?"

"Two."

"And how long has he been off colour?"

"He hasn't been himself for a couple of days, a bit grizzly and off his food. I thought he was teething but today he has been worse and this afternoon he became very feverish."

That he was feverish there was no doubt. I didn't need to take his temperature; he was flushed and felt very hot. I proceeded to give him a thorough examination. No neck stiffness, ears fine, throat a little red, tummy seemed soft but as he didn't really like me examining him at all I couldn't be certain. His chest was clear. I didn't have a diagnosis. What a pity I hadn't done my sick children's job before I had done this job.

"So what's wrong, Doctor?"

"I can't find anything other than he's got a fever."

"Well we know that, Doctor, but why has he got a fever?"

"I don't know."

"Well that's not much help; what do we do?"

"I want you to tepid sponge him to bring his temperature down. Encourage him to drink; it doesn't matter if he doesn't eat. If you can, catch a sample of his pee, please. I will come back in the morning and see him again. It's almost certainly an infection and he should be better in a day or so." And with nothing more to say I left the house. I realised that I hadn't inspired confidence, but how could I when I didn't feel confident myself.

The following morning I returned to number thirty-seven. Mary's husband was away to work, a fact that I welcomed; I had the feeling that he could have been difficult to deal with.

"What sort of a night did you have with Jamie, Mary?"

"He took a while to settle but once he did he slept most of the night, but this morning he's been feverish again and irritable. I'm sorry I couldn't catch a sample when he peed; it just went over everything but not in the bottle."

"No, it can be difficult I know." That was a complete lie as in hospital I never had to get the sample, the nurses did that, and in any case, we weren't dealing with children in adult hospitals. I examined Jamie as I had done the previous evening and there was nothing new. "There's nothing new. I'm afraid you will just have to be patient. Continue with tepid sponging when he gets hot and encourage him to drink. I'll look in tomorrow."

I worried all day about Jamie. Medicine is not so difficult when you know what's wrong with someone. Have a diagnosis and you know what to do but without a diagnosis it's not so easy. That was a lesson I was beginning to learn; maybe general practice wasn't quite so easy after all! The rest of the day passed without any further trouble, that is until nine that evening, when the phone rang.

"Hello, Doctor Neville speaking."

"Hello, Doctor Prentice here, we met briefly at the surgery this morning. I have just been phoned by a Mr Weir requesting a visit for his son; apparently you have been seeing him."

"Yes that's true."

"Well they are very dissatisfied with you and want me to go round now and see the boy."

"Oh I'm sorry." I was cut short.

"I have no intention of going but you had better go and sort your problem out before they put in a formal complaint. Good night." And the line went dead.

"What was that all about, darling?" my wife asked, putting down her knitting.

"It's about the wee boy I mentioned at supper. The father rang another doctor because he wasn't satisfied with me."

"That's not very nice."

"No, and the other doctor wasn't very nice either. I can't say I blame the father. I would be worried if the boy was mine. The trouble is I think my anxiety is obvious to them. I will have to learn how to appear confident even when I'm not. Any idea what I should do?"

"Not really, but you will obviously have to go round now."

"Yes, of course, but what do you think I should do if the wee boy is just the same?"

"Well, either send him into hospital or, if you think he doesn't need to go in, tell them you will ask for a second opinion from a consultant paediatrician tomorrow. Patients love second opinions."

"Darling, you are a star, that's just what I'll do, thank you." I kissed my wife affectionately and set off for thirty-seven.

I rang the bell and Mr Weir opened it. His startled expression was accompanied by an expletive. "What the hell are you doing here? I asked Doctor Prentice to come; he has a good reputation."

"He phoned me and said I was to come as he certainly wasn't going to," I replied slightly defensively.

"All right, I suppose you had better come in." He turned and I followed him inside.

"Mary, I'm afraid it's Doctor Neville again, Doctor Prentice refused to come."

Feeling totally unwelcome and indeed disliked, I turned to Mary. "How is Jamie?"

"He's been pretty miserable all day and not eaten anything. He has taken several bottles and I have caught some of his pee for you."

"Well done, I see he has fallen asleep and he doesn't feel so hot."

"He has only just fallen off after we phoned Doctor Prentice."

"Good I'll try not to wake him, but I want to check him over again."

I managed, without waking him, to check that he didn't have a stiff neck, his ears were fine and, after warming the stethoscope and listening to his chest, his breathing was fine.

"So, what do you think this time, Doctor, or do you still not know?" asked Mr Weir rather sarcastically.

"Mr Weir, I have decided that what I have advised, namely fluids and tepid sponging, is the correct treatment, but if tomorrow morning Jamie is not better I will request a second opinion from a consultant paediatrician."

"And what's that?"

"A doctor who specialises in children's illnesses; I'll be back in the morning."

"I start my morning shift at eight thirty," said Mr Weir, "and if Jamie has to go to hospital I will want to be with him, so you will need to come before eight." No please, no thank you, just 'come'.

I turned and left. The door banged behind me.

"How did you get on; did my suggestion work?" enquired my wife as soon as I was in the door.

"Yes, well I hope so. They weren't very happy but I felt more confident and that may have been because I thought the wee fellow was a bit better. Time will tell."

The following morning I rose early, had a shower, dressed and had a quick cup of coffee and departed once again for number thirty-seven. I decided to take complete charge of the situation and stand no more truck from Mr Weir. I rang the bell and, without waiting, opened the front door and strode purposefully into the house and on into the kitchen.

"Good morning, Doctor," uttered Mary and William almost in unison. William stood up from the table. "Do sit down, Doctor."

"How's Jamie, what sort of a night did he have?" I asked.

"Wonderful, he slept all night and look at him now." They pointed to a playpen hidden behind a settee. I knelt on the settee and looked over; there he was surrounded by a pile of coloured bricks. He looked up and smiled. I will never be more relieved however long I live. I may see equally welcoming smiles, and I hope I do, but never ever will I see one that gave me such relief.

"He doesn't need to see the patrician, does he?" said Mr Weir.

"The paediatrician," I corrected him, "no, he doesn't," I replied with, I must admit, a relieved smile.

"Oh, Doctor, thank you so much, you've been wonderful," said Mary. I smiled.

"Doctor, I owe you an apology," said William. "I'm so sorry I have been rude to you and I thought you didn't know what was wrong with Jamie and you were right all the time. It was as you said an infection. I don't know how you doctors can tell what is wrong with someone when they can't tell you how they are feeling. Looking after small children must be like looking after dogs: they can't tell you either, can they?"

"You are quite right, William, it can be difficult." I felt first names were now appropriate.

"Doctor, I want to give you a present."

"Oh, there is no need for that."

"But there is." He produced a tin of tobacco and offered it to me.

"That's very kind but I don't smoke."

"Oh it's not 'baccy' in the tin; it's fish bait. I see you have a trout fly in the lapel of your jacket. It's a Peter Ross I think, so I knew you were a fisherman like me. This bait is deadly, much better than flies but don't let the water bailiff catch you with it. Now, Doctor, I'm sorry I must fly to work, it's been a privilege to meet you." So saying, he shook my hand and left.

I turned to Mary. "I think you should have no more trouble; Jamie is obviously a lot better but if you have any worries don't hesitate to give me a ring. I'm here for another ten days."

"Thank you so much, Doctor, I don't know what we'll do when you go. Could you not join Doctor Norman's practice?"

I smiled again, shook hands, and left. Maybe general practice was worth doing after all.

A rash mistake

Before I tell you about another of my mistakes, let me explain how a doctor's day was constructed. Back in the '50s and '60s home visits were the norm and it was not unusual for all the partners, and any assistant that happened to be available, to do at least ten visits in the town in the morning, a surgery from one thirty till three p.m. and then country visits till four thirty p.m. with an evening surgery till around seven p.m. One partner would then stay on duty until eight thirty the following morning. We would then all meet at the surgery (including the poor chap who had been on duty overnight) and discuss any problems that we had encountered the previous day; we would then allocate the visits that were requested or required.

Most visits were follow-up visits just to make sure the patient was improving. The country visits were done in the afternoon, each valley being done by a different doctor, so you would probably only see three or four people in the hour and a half. All the farm cottages contained farm workers and were not holiday homes which so many are today as a result of the advent of hour-saving combine harvesters, quad bikes and so on. Most of the country patients did not have cars but did have several children, so a good deal of time was spent attending to the rural population. As an assistant I was the ideal chap to have around if a distant visit had been requested. One afternoon my senior partner, assuming I was not busy, though whether or not I was didn't seem to matter, asked me to visit a farmer who lived some ten miles away. "You know how to get there, Peter?" he asked.

"No, sir," I replied.

"Dead easy, you can't go wrong. At the end of the High Street take the left exit and go on for about ten miles and the farm is on your left. Decent chap, the farmer, never bothers us, but apparently he's covered in spots, sounds interesting. Let me know how you get on."

"Yes, sir." I didn't like the sound of it. Dermatology was not my strongest suit, indeed the more I saw in general practice the more I realised I didn't have many strong suits. I set off and, as instructed, took the left exit at the end of the High Street. Sadly, what my senior partner had omitted to tell me was that there were two other exits before I reached the main road to Carlisle; they were so minor he obviously didn't think them worth mentioning. After ten miles up this fairly narrow road, I met a wide farm vehicle and had no option but to stop. I jumped out and asked the tractor man if there was anywhere nearby where one of us could get off the road. He suggested I reverse back until I came to an open gate in a field, that apparently was where he was going. "By the way," I said. "Is Teviot Farm near here?"

He shook his head. "No, you'd best to go to Hawick and then turn left down the A7 and go on for about ten miles. You can't miss it."

My heart sank. I was now running late and was supposed to be back for evening surgery at four thirty. I reversed the car for about a quarter of a mile, turned at an open gate, accelerated back to Hawick, found the main road and headed for Teviot Farm. I found the farm without any further difficulty, stopped outside the front door and rang the bell.

A smiling middle-aged lady opened the door. "Ah, you'll be the new doctor, kind of you to come. I trust you had no difficulty finding us?"

"Oh no, fine, no problem." Well there didn't seem any point in telling the truth.

"My husband is in bed. He really is most uncomfortable; he will be pleased to see you." I followed her upstairs to the bedroom. "Here's the doctor for you, Sandy." I held out my hand and introduced myself.

"Oh, I wouldn't advise shaking my hand, Doctor, just look at the mess I'm in; it might be smittle." That was a new word to me and I wasn't quite sure whether it was the name of a disease I had never heard of or some local dialect.

He was right; he was in a mess. Hundreds, or possibly thousands, of spots covered his body; many had obviously been scratched until they bled. I had never seen anything like it.

"Well, Doctor, what do you think, am I going to live?" He laughed and I tried to laugh too. The problem was I didn't know what to say.

Clutching at straws I asked him, "Have you been in contact with any animals lately?" A more stupid question to a farmer would be hard to think of!

"Only the same ones as I have for the last thirty years."

"Yes, of course, but I meant any new ones."

"No."

"Have you been dipping the sheep?" I remembered my uncle getting a rash after dipping his sheep when I had had a holiday on his farm. Maybe he was allergic to something.

"No."

"Been in the hen house recently?"

"Well now you mention it, I have been lately. Could that be the problem?"

"Yes," I replied clutching at another straw. "Yes I think it's hen fleas."

"Hen fleas, I've never heard of that. Can you do anything for them or rather me?"

"Yes certainly, I recommend you cover all the spots with calamine lotion. There is no need to stay in bed; too many people die in bed," and I gave a hollow laugh.

"Thank you, Doctor, you really have surprised me. Still you're the one who is the expert not me. Thank you for coming."

I smiled, said goodbye and with a sense of relief, left the farm.

The following morning at our eight thirty meeting I was asked about my visit to the farmer by my senior partner. "How did you get on, Peter? Found your way all right?"

"Yes, sir," I lied.

"Nice fellow, isn't he? What was wrong with him?"

"I think the rash was due to hen fleas."

"Really, most unusual, never heard of that. Thank goodness you went as I would never have thought of that."

About two days later one of the other partners had occasion to go up the Teviot valley so I asked him, if he had time, would he pop in and see the farmer just to make sure my treatment was working.

"No problem, Peter, I'll have plenty time as I've only a couple of other visits."

I hesitate to tell you the rest of this tale so please keep it to yourself. You see it's a bit embarrassing!

Later that evening after the surgery had finished, there was a knock on my consulting room door. "Come in," I said.

"Not interrupting you I hope?" and in walked the partner who had been up Teviot.

"No, how did you get on? Did my treatment help the farmer?"

"Oh yes, he is much better."

"Oh I am glad. To be honest, I wasn't absolutely sure of my diagnosis."

"You were nearly right. You said: 'hen fleas' but actually it was 'chickenpox'. Have you ever seen chickenpox before?"

"No."

"Well you will know the next time. No harm done. Goodnight."

"Goodnight," I replied. Now it must surely amaze the reader that I was so stupid, but in my defence hear me out. As a student in hospital we never saw any of the infectious diseases: mumps, measles and of course chickenpox, are never admitted to hospital. I expect we were shown slides at a dermatology lecture which was held after lunch. They were badly attended and if one did go, there was a tendency, when the lights went out and the slide show began, to either slip out of the side door of the lecture hall or fall asleep.

Anyway, that's my excuse but not quite the end of this embarrassing tale. I immediately bought an expensive book of *Skin Disorders* beautifully illustrated so that in future if I were to be faced with an unusual rash (which I was) I could slip out to the car, under some pretence of having forgotten something, and have a quick look at my text book and find an equivalent picture to the rash I had been called to see. Anyway, hens and chickens are much the same, aren't they?

Let sleeping dogs lie

They say, well some people say, that the longer you live together the more alike you become. That is surely true as far as behaviour is concerned but surely not physically... and yet I am not so sure.

When I was a recently qualified doctor, I took a job as an assistant for a year in a busy practice in the south of Scotland. The senior partner, Doctor Wilson, (there were two other junior partners,) was an amiable elderly gentleman who had built up a good practice, and I am sure had worked hard, but now decided it was time to ease up and reap the harvest. If the weather was cold, or wet, or snowy, he preferred to stay inside. "It's my rheumatism," he would say or "It's that shrapnel, they should have removed it," referring to an old war wound. He would see half a dozen patients between ten a.m. and twelve p.m. in his consulting room, which incidentally doubled up as his dining room, and then would have a break. He looked upon me as his personal assistant and the other two partners were not expected to ask me to do anything unless I was 'unemployed' (by him). I liked him and being young and enthusiastic and prepared to cure the world, did not mind being taken advantage of.

His knowledge of his patients was phenomenal. He was close on eighty years old and had been in the practice for the best part of fifty years. That meant that he would often have looked after three generations and probably even four, and believe it or not, probably delivered them all. No wonder he needed a rest. Whenever he asked me to pay a visit to one of his patients, he would give me a complete briefing on their past health and other information that he felt was both interesting and occasionally even useful; there was nothing he didn't know about their health, wealth or love life. He was a remarkable man.

One day when I reported to his surgery at twelve p.m. precisely, having done several house visits, he was in one of his skittish moods. "Ah, Peter, I've a really interesting visit for you today. Not too busy I hope."

It wasn't a question and made no difference whether I was or not. "No, sir."

"Good, excellent, we don't want to work you too hard, do we? There's a call in for the Roberts which I would like you to deal with. I would go but my rheumatism is playing up; I think it's the cold weather. I don't think you've met them, have you?" He looked up and smiled.

"No, sir," I replied waiting for one of his customary family histories to follow.

"Let me fill you in. Do sit down. They are a delightful pair; been married fifty years, no, more, nearly sixty, I think. Well anyway they are in their eighties. They are a bit like twins, even look a bit alike. They never used to; she was a bonnie lass, but he was always a bit overweight and untidy. They are both untidy now, indeed the house is the scruffiest house you will ever have seen, and maybe ever will see in your life. I give you a tip, leave your coat in the car because there will be nowhere to lay it and whatever you do don't kneel on the floor." Why I should want to kneel on the floor I had no idea. He was a strange old man, but I liked him.

"Good heavens, is that the time? I've kept you too long. Sorry about that. I'll hear tomorrow how you got on. They live at Valley View about three miles up the road to Newcastleton, you can't miss it. Morag in the surgery will show you on the map."

"Fine, thanks for all the information I can't wait to meet them." And I meant it.

The Roberts lived in a detached cottage. I think it must have been a roadman's dwelling at some time, but now that roadmen no longer exist, it had been sold off. It was raining hard and as I got out of the car, I pulled my coat collar up, put my hat on and hurried up the garden path. It was covered in weeds and puddles; I felt the water seep into my nice black brogues; maybe I should wear wellies for country visits. I rang the bell and waited. I rang it again then opened the door. "It's behind the door," came a voice from within.

"What's behind the door?" I replied. At that moment an old lady appeared. "Oh sorry I thought you were the man from the electric to read the meter. Are you the new doctor?"

"Yes. Mrs Roberts, I presume?" In a strange funny way I was reminded of Stanley's famous greeting of Doctor Livingston all those years ago!

"Yes, do come in and it's Bessie. Mike is in bed."

I followed Bessie into the bedroom but really, I think it was the living room.

"Ah, Doctor, very good to meet you. I'm Mike." We shook hands. "Doctor Wilson said he would send you. I think he should retire; he's getting a bit old. Good doctor mind, but getting too old." I looked round the room and took stock. Doctor Wilson was right. I have never seen such a chaotic, untidy, shambolic room. Apart from the double bed in the middle of the room there were two easy chairs and a small sofa. Bessie was now sitting down on one chair and a large black Labrador on the other. Half the sofa was occupied by a large pile of newspapers and magazines and on the other half lay a tray with what I assume were the breakfast dishes. Leaning against the sofa was a bicycle. It had, I think, been there some time as both the front and the rear tyres were flat.

"So who's the cyclist?" I said smiling enquiringly at both in turn.

"Ah, yes, I used to, but not now," said Mike. "I am going to put it in the garage, but I'll need to tidy that first. Remind me to do that, Bessie, when I get better."

43

I lay down my bag and took my coat off; a voice in my head said 'leave your coat in the car'. I looked around for somewhere to put it. Eventually I decided to balance it on the edge of the sofa. "Now, Mike, what's the problem?"

"I think it's the mushrooms, Doctor. I picked a lot yesterday and Bessie makes the best mushroom soup, but I think I must have given her a rogue one. I've had rumblings and tummy pains and diarrhoea all night. Poor Bessie couldn't sleep for the noise. Isn't that right, Bessie?"

"Yes, you sounded like an outboard motor," she said with a laugh.

"Really," I said wondering when she had last heard an outboard motor.

I looked at Mike; he had a slight smile which struggled out from his straggly beard which covered much of his chin and cheeks. He didn't look in any pain despite the rumblings which were clearly audible. "Well let's have a look at your tummy." So saying, I knelt down beside the bed, as I had been taught to do when examining the abdomen. The voice in my ear returned: 'don't kneel on the floor'. I felt something moist seep through my trouser and round my knee. It was too late now. I put my hand under his duvet and felt his tummy. It was soft and obviously not tender.

"Well, Doc, will I live a little longer?" he enquired and laughed just like his wife.

"Yes, long enough to fix the bike and the garage. You're absolutely right I think, the mushrooms are the cause of your problem. I suggest you eat nothing for a couple of days, drink plenty, but not alcohol."

"Yes, no whisky, Mike," said Bessie from behind her knitting.

I looked up; she was smiling and shaking her head. "No whisky for you today, young man." She had a lovely smile and must in her early years have been quite a beauty, but autumn had come and with it her looks had sadly faded and the odd straggly wisp of hair sprouted from her chin and ears, a bit like Mike really.

"Well thanks for coming, Doctor," they said almost in unison.

"Not at all, I'm glad it's nothing worse. It's a pleasure to meet you both. I'll let myself out. Bye."

"Bye, Doctor, thank you."

I put on my coat, picked up my bag, struggled past the bike and departed the cottage. As I reached the car, I put my hand in my coat pocket to retrieve my car keys. I felt something sticky. I looked down and there, stuck half way in and halfway out of my coat pocket, was a half-eaten jam sandwich. I had a lot to learn about how to practise medicine which I wouldn't find in a text book.

About three weeks later Doctor Wilson rang me. "Peter, be a good chap and pop in again and see Mike Roberts; Bessie says he's got a bad tummy again. I think you made quite a hit with them last time, otherwise I would have gone."

I smiled to myself… time the old boy retired.

As before it was raining heavily when I made my way to Valley View, but this time I was prepared. I left my coat in the car and strode confidently up the path in my new welly boots. I rang the bell, opened the door calling, "It's just me," and walked in almost falling over the bicycle which was propped up in the short corridor that led to the main room. "Morning, been at the mushrooms again?"

"Morning, Doctor," they replied almost in unison.

"Hope you noticed Mike has removed the bike?"

"Yes, Bessie, I did." I smiled benignly. "Well, Mike, is it the usual mushroom trouble?"

"Well I've got the rumbles and tummy pains but no diarrhoea this time."

I looked at him from the foot of the bed; it was different this time. The duvet which lay across him was heaped up and even I could hear the rumblings. I realised that we had a potentially more dangerous problem. I remembered the surgeon's lecture: 'If the tummy swells and the bowels don't move, and the bowel sounds are loud you can bet your bottom dollar you have an intestinal obstruction, so don't delay'.

"Let me have a look at you, Mike. Put out your tongue, please." Actually, it was fine. I took his pulse. "Fine, now let's have a look at your tummy," and without kneeling down I slipped a hand under the duvet again. I will never forget the shock I got from what happened next. What I'm about to tell you is the absolute truth. I doubt if I will ever again witness such an event if I practise as long as Doctor Wilson, indeed I doubt if he will ever have had such an experience. A Labrador jumped out from under the duvet. The swelling and the rumblings disappeared across the room and settled on the sofa.

"Good God!" I shouted.

"Sorry to give you a fright, Doc," Mike said.

"Now, let me check your tummy again. Seems fine to me. Not tender?"

"No."

"Good, I don't think there's anything serious going on. Like last time just stay on fluids for twenty-four hours and I think your tummy will settle down."

"Thanks, Doctor. Oh, Bessie has a wee something for you. She made it herself."

Bessie gave me a small parcel. I thanked her and with a wave of my hand took my leave. I put the parcel on the front seat and drove off. When I got home after the evening surgery, I gave my wife the parcel. "I was given this by a patient today, homemade she said. I don't know what it is." My wife took the parcel through to the kitchen. As I wasn't on duty that night, I poured myself a generous gin and tonic. "Do you want a drink, darling," I shouted to my wife.

"Yes please, the usual."

47

I poured her a large dry sherry and took it through to the kitchen. I then returned to the sitting room and, picking up the local paper and my G & T, sank back contentedly in my chair. Yes, general practice was certainly interesting.

"Darling, are you hungry?"

"Yes, why?"

"Well I was planning just haggis, neeps and tatties."

"Yes, that's fine"

"Well, could you manage soup as well? That kind patient has made some mushroom soup and it smells delicious."

"No thanks, I'll just stick to the haggis. I wouldn't advise you to touch the soup." And, smiling to myself, I sipped my gin.

A fishy tale

Johnny Pascal, or 'Rascal' as he became known to anyone who had dealings with him, was best avoided. He seemed to cause trouble wherever he went – and the trouble was that he usually managed to escape squeaky clean. However, those involved with him ended up taking all the blame. His idea of telling the truth depended entirely on what he thought he could get away with; he had absolutely no loyalty to his friends and, to be perfectly honest, that was why he had very few and they were best avoided. He had a delightful mother who was too kind to cope and a father who had the embarrassment of being in the police force and just shook his head when it came to Johnny. An older brother seemed to have inherited all the brains and was a student studying to be a doctor at Edinburgh University and a sister was a Divinity student, also in Edinburgh.

I had heard a lot about Pascal but hadn't ever met him, that is until one evening in early October. The salmon were running and the water bailiffs were busy trying to keep one step ahead of the poachers, an almost impossible task. My phone rang just as I was finishing my supper. "It's the cottage hospital on the phone for you, darling," my wife called from the sitting room. I downed the last mouthful of apple crumble and went through to the sitting room. I took the phone from my wife.

"Hello."

"Hello, Doctor, Sister Green here. I have young Johnny Pascal here, with a most unusual hand injury. I'm afraid you will have to come; I've never seen anything quite like it."

"Okay, I'll be up shortly."

Sister Green was right; it was a bizarre injury. Pascal had a two foot long thin piece of wood stuck up his sleeve; attached to the end which was sticking out below his shirt cuff was part of a large metal hook, about two inches long, which had been spliced onto the wooden stick. The problem was the hook was imbedded into the palm of his hand just below his thumb. It was of course a cleek, also known as a gaff – *a crude hook on the end of a stick used to catch a salmon, highly illegal and of course cruel.*

"Well, well, Johnny, what's the story this time?"

"I was cycling along the road when I hit a pot hole and as I was holding the handle bars the jarring resulted in the hook imbedding itself in my hand. I did try to pull it out, but it wouldn't budge and in any case it was too sore."

"No, you can't pull a hook out because the barb on it won't allow it to go back the way it went in," I explained.

"So what can I do? I'm supposed to be in court tomorrow and I can't go like this; I will just have to call off."

"What are you there for this time, Johnny?"

"Oh, nothing much, they think I was the person who broke into the wine shop in the High Street. Crazy, I don't drink, but they don't listen."

"The good news is," I said, "I will be able to remove the hook and the bad news is you will be able to go to court tomorrow. What I will do is this: I will freeze the skin around the hook with some local anaesthetic and then push the hook in until the point comes out through another hole in the skin; do you follow what I mean?"

"Yes, I've heard that before but never seen it done. Then what?"

"Then I will cut off the barb and then draw the hook back the way it went in. Now you lie back, relax and I will get on with the job."

Having injected the area with local anaesthetic, I had no difficulty in pushing the barb out. The snag was I couldn't cut it off; it was too thick. I rang for Sister.

"Have we got a hacksaw, Sister? This hook is too thick for me to be able to cut it with scissors."

"Yes, but it's very old. I don't know when it was last used."

"Please boil it up, Sister. It obviously needs to be sterilised and we will see if it works."

Well it did work, but not before Johnny had passed out with fright when he saw me start to saw away at the hook. Then I withdrew very easily the now barbless hook. Next, I removed the hook from the stick and finally was able to pull the stick out from his sleeve. "Hey presto, how's that, Johnny?" I said triumphantly, "I feel a bit like a magician completing a piece of sleight of hand, if you get what I mean?" I don't think Johnny saw the joke.

"Is it all over?" He looked up anxiously.

"Yes. Sister, please give Johnny a glass of water."

"Can I have the hook and stick back, please?" he asked rather pathetically.

"You can have the stick but that's all. Sister, please put on a small dressing. Is your tetanus up to date, Johnny?"

"Yes, I cut my other hand on a barbed fence last month and was given an injection for tetanus then."

Probably running away from the bailiffs. I decided not to enquire further.

"Pop into the surgery in a week and let me check the wound. OK?"

"Thanks, Doc."

"Pleasure."

I didn't actually expect Johnny to attend the surgery the following week, but I was wrong; he did.

"How is it?"

"Fine."

"Good, let's have a look." I took the dressing off and am glad to say the small wound was well healed and the hand was not tender. "Good, don't do it again."

52

"Don't worry, Doc, I've learnt my lesson. By the way I've left a small parcel for you with reception. Thanks, Doc, cheerio." I went to the front desk to see what he'd left. A parcel, well something wrapped in a newspaper actually, lay on the table and sticking out of one end was the tail of a fish. I hastily removed the parcel and took it back to my consulting room and put it on the floor under my examination couch. I then called the next patient.

"Sergeant Pascal, please."

"Evening, Doctor, is Johnny all right? I saw him leave just as I arrived, but I didn't get a chance to speak to him. Nothing serious I hope."

"No, no, just a routine check-up, you'll be due one soon."

"Yes, that's why I'm in. I think my tetanus is due and I don't want to take any chances. I had a fall two weeks ago chasing a couple of poachers and cut my hand, not bad enough to need a stitch, but I wondered if my tetanus was up to date. These poachers are a damn nuisance."

"Yes they must be. Now pull up your left sleeve, please."

"By the way, Doctor, I hope you don't mind me mentioning it, but I think you must have trouble with your drains; there's a funny fishy sort of smell in here."

"Yes, you are quite right the plumber was in this afternoon and is coming later this evening; apparently there is a blocked drain."

53

"Oh good, I hope you didn't mind me mentioning it."

"Not at all."

"Bye, Doctor, many thanks. Must fly; we've got a cunning plan tonight."

"What for?"

"To catch the poachers of course. Not something I suppose you'll be bothered with."

"No you're right. Are they locals or outsiders?"

"Oh, almost certainly outsiders, we are too smart for the locals, they wouldn't risk it. They know we would catch them."

"Yes, I suppose so," I replied innocently.

A crying shame

Jennifer Wright and her husband Duncan lived in a terraced house that had been built just after the war. Initially they had rented it, but after the Right to Buy came about in the early eighties, they bought it. They were on the ground floor and had neighbours on both sides and in the flat above them. This is relevant as you will discover. Jennifer had been a receptionist at one of the surgeries in Galashiels and Duncan was a policeman. They had joined my list when they married and moved to Hawick in the early seventies. I well remember the day I first met Jennifer. She had come to the practice with her cards and asked if she and her husband could join our list.

"You don't mind us coming from Galashiels?" she said with a twinkle in her eye and a bewitching smile, which I was to discover rarely left her face.

"No, of course not," I replied, remembering the friendly rivalry between the two towns. "At least you are both from the same town, so we can't call it a mixed marriage." She laughed, and so started a friendship which grew apace. She was in her late thirties and Duncan the same. They had been married for nearly twenty years, she said, but had no children. This I thought was unusual and made a note to study their health records when they eventually arrived from the health office in Galashiels.

"Duncan has made an appointment to see you on Tuesday afternoon; like me he's fighting fit, so I hope we won't trouble you." She smiled and held my gaze.

"I'm sure you won't." I felt quite bewitched.

Within a year Duncan was promoted to sergeant and Jennifer applied and was appointed as a receptionist at the cottage hospital. I saw her frequently, as I visited the cottage every day, but rarely at the surgery as Jennifer was seldom ill. When I did see her it was always for the same problem 'a missed period'. Poor Jennifer, her periods were always irregular; often having a gap of ten weeks between one and the next, and the pregnancy tests were always negative. One evening I was making a late visit to the cottage to see an elderly gentleman who I had admitted earlier in the day. As I walked in the front door I nearly knocked Jennifer over as she was coming out. "Oh sorry, Jennifer. You're working late; it's time you were home; it's nearly eight o'clock."

"I was just sorting some patient records. Actually, I have an appointment to see you tomorrow."

"Good I'll look forward to seeing you then. Good night, Jennifer."

Jennifer duly appeared the following morning. She opened the conversation. "You will probably laugh at me, but I think I'm pregnant." She smiled and looked just a trifle embarrassed.

"Oh Jennifer, we've been down that road so often before with no success. I think it's doubtful, for you are, what, forty-two now, and whilst that's not impossible it's certainly very unlikely."

"Well, actually I'm forty-four; I feel different this time."

"In what way?"

"I can't stop eating."

"But that's the opposite of what I would expect."

"I know, but it's odd. I eat two or three Kit Kats a day!" and Jennifer blushed.

"That is certainly odd. When was your last period?"

"Ten weeks ago, but as you know I only have one every ten or twelve weeks. Anyway, I've brought a specimen and hope you don't mind sending it off."

"Of course I don't. I'll see the girls send it off tomorrow."

"Oh, you are kind, Doctor. I know I am being a bit daft but I feel different this time. I know it's unlikely but well… you never know. I wonder, Doctor, if you could send it off with a different name; I know the girls at the desk so well I don't want them to know."

"That's easy," I replied. "We will call you Debbie Thomas; how does that sound?"

"Not 'Doubting Thomas' I hope. Goodnight and thank you." She stood up, swayed slightly, and left. She surely hadn't been drinking or maybe she was pregnant after all. Oh, I hoped so. I finished my paperwork, filled

57

out the forms for the laboratory and put them and the specimen jar in the out tray for the morning collection.

When I came in on the Monday, Jennifer was already sitting in the waiting room.

I hurried through to my consulting room and buzzed for my first patient. It was Jennifer. She looked at me enquiringly; she didn't need to ask. I said nothing; I just shook my head sadly. "Thank you, Doctor, sorry to have troubled you." And without another word rose from her seat and left the room. I completed my morning surgery with difficulty. I couldn't concentrate. Life wasn't fair; there was me just having to look at my wife and she was 'off to the races' again, and here was Jennifer married for twenty years and unable to conceive. I dictated a few letters, and then as usual, went up to the cottage. Jennifer was sitting at her desk.

"Jennifer, could I have a private word for a minute."

"Of course," she turned to her colleague, "Betty, could you cover for me for a minute; Doctor needs me."

We went into a small interview room. "I'm so sorry, Jennifer. Is there any way I can help?"

"It's not your fault, Doctor, in fact it's not anyone's fault."

"What did Duncan say?"

"Oh, I didn't tell him that I thought I might be pregnant; it wouldn't have been fair."

"No, I daresay you're right but a trouble shared... well, you know what I mean."

"Yes."

"Is there anything I can do? Would you like to take some time off?"

"Yes, I would. Do you think matron will mind? Duncan is off next week and we need to get away and have time together to talk; we really do need to."

"I'll sign you off for two weeks and I'm sure matron won't mind; I know she thinks the world of you; well we all do. Will that suit?"

"Yes, thank you, Doctor, I'm most grateful."

"Right, off you go." I stood up and Jennifer gave a sad smile and left.

Jennifer did come back to work a fortnight later. I was looking forward to seeing her at the cottage but when I got there on the Monday morning she was nowhere to be seen. I asked Betty if she had seen Jennifer. "Yes she was in at eight thirty but looked awful and had to go home."

"Thank you. I will pay a house call and see what the problem is."

I finished my work at the hospital and drove to Jennifer's house, knocked on the door and without waiting opened it. "It's just me," I shouted. "May I come in?"

"Please come in, Doctor, I'm in bed."

I hurried along the narrow corridor and pushed open the bedroom door. Jennifer was lying in bed clutching a sick bowl. She looked up with a strained expression. "Doctor, are you sure I'm not pregnant? I can't eat anything. I couldn't eat anything on holiday, not even

Kit Kats, and I feel light headed and, well, just not myself at all. Duncan says it must be the change of life. Oh, Doctor, I can't go on like this."

I sat on the bed and held her hand. "Jennifer, I want to examine you. I think you might well be pregnant. I may not be able to tell because you might only be a few weeks but let's see." I took the sick basin from her and she lay back. "I'll just go down to the car and get my bag… won't be seconds."

I examined Jennifer and, reluctantly, couldn't come to a definite conclusion. "I'm not sure, physically it's too early to tell, but my guess, for what it's worth, is that you are pregnant. Get Duncan to bring in a specimen tomorrow and I will send it off. In all the times previously when you've missed a period you have not been like this."

"But I'm forty-four!"

"I know, I know, but stranger things have happened."

"Have you ever had a forty-four year old before?" she asked almost pleadingly.

"No, but I've never had a Kit Kat eater. Jennifer, I honestly think you are pregnant."

"Doctor, would you do something for me please?"

"Yes, of course."

"Hand me the sick basin quickly; you put it on the dressing table."

I handed her the bowl and she promptly vomited. Shortly after I left.

I sent the specimen off in the morning and waited impatiently for the result; it came on Thursday. It was *positive*.

I picked up the phone on my desk. "Jennifer, it's positive – you are pregnant."

Seven months later Malcolm was delivered by caesarean section. He weighed six and a half pounds. I'm tempted to end the tale here because it's such a happy place to do so, but then the whole point of why I started it would be lost and in any case the end was not what I expected.

Malcolm was breastfed and thrived, meeting all his required development targets. One day Jennifer, who had taken six months off, came to see me.

"Doctor, I can't go on like this. I'm at the end of my tether."

"Why, what on earth is wrong?" I asked. I must say she looked a shadow of her normal self – tired, drawn and, for once, there was no smile. I doubted if she had brushed her hair and she looked as if she had dressed in a hurry.

"It's Malcolm – he won't sleep. He is fine during the day, a real joy, but when I put him down at night he howls. If I go through to him he stops at once and smiles and is as happy as Sam, but as soon as I leave him it all starts again. Duncan and I can't take much more of this."

"Yes, it's a common problem but don't worry we can soon sort it for you," I said optimistically. "Now listen carefully. Malcolm is like anyone else, he just doesn't like being shut away from what's going on, so this is what you are to do. When he is ready for bed take him to his cot and go through your usual routine. Then say 'goodnight' and turn the light off and shut the door."

"Yes, I do all that, but he just starts crying again."

"Well, you must be strong and leave him to cry himself to sleep."

"And how long can I safely leave him to cry?"

"Until he stops," I said emphatically.

"It's easy for you to say that; you live in a big house and your nearest neighbours are miles away and can't hear anyone crying. Mine are so close, I think they must be thinking I'm abusing the child." Jennifer was almost cross with me.

"I'm sure they don't but I take your point, so go and see them and tell them the problem and say: 'my doctor has told me to let Malcolm cry, so please don't be worried when you hear him'."

"All right, I'll try it and see what happens. Thanks, Doctor."

Three days later Jennifer returned. "Doctor, it's no good. I think you should take Malcolm into care; I'm terrified I'm going to hurt him. I did what you suggested but eventually I had to go in to him, and it took a while for him to settle."

I thought for a moment and decided that Jennifer was indeed at risk of doing something dangerous; she was very agitated and definitely needed some sort of tranquilizer to settle her down. She needed a good sleep and if we could get her to sleep well for a few nights and stop her going in to Malcolm, I was sure Malcolm would develop a normal sleeping pattern. "Jennifer, I understand exactly how you're feeling."

"I doubt it," she said in a most uncharacteristic way, "but go on."

"I think a small sedative is necessary. Use one of these sleeping pills every night. Make an appointment to see me after three nights but if you feel you are at breaking point, ring me. You promise?"

"Yes, thank you, sorry to be a pest but I feel better after talking about it." She gave me a half smile, picked up the small envelope with the three sleeping pills and left. I heaved a sigh, not of relief but a mixture of anxiety and apprehension. I understood how young mums could get so close to harming their babies.

Jennifer returned as promised in three days and I did not need to ask how things had gone: her smile lit up her face; her hair was beautifully swept back in a ponytail. "Doctor, you're a genius; Malcolm slept like a log and when I went to check him for the first time before going to bed he was fast asleep cuddling his bear and looked angelic. And I'll tell you something else, he didn't wake in the night for a feed. Yes, Doctor, you are a genius."

"And how did you sleep; equally well I hope?"

"Yes, no problem. May I have some more sleeping pills, please? They are wonderful?"

"Well I'll give you half a dozen, but I don't want you to get hooked on sleeping pills so please keep them for a rainy day and keep them away from Malcolm because they would be dangerous if he got hold of them."

Jennifer went white. "But, Doctor, I thought the three you gave me were for him!"

"Good God no! Heavens, you didn't give Malcolm them, did you?"

"Yes, one a night, just as you said."

"Oh, Jennifer, I'm sorry. I obviously didn't explain things properly; the sleeping pills were for you to get a good sleep and hopefully stop you going into Malcolm's bedroom."

"Well, you must admit they worked, didn't they? I suppose you won't be giving me the other six." She smiled mischievously. "I won't need them anyway; I'm off to buy some ear plugs." She rose from her chair, shook hands and left.

Jennifer resumed her work at the cottage the following week.

I should add that what I have written here is absolutely true, except for the fact that Jennifer didn't actually work at the cottage and, of course, the names in the story were not the real names. But I suppose someone, somewhere, if she reads this, will recognise who Jennifer is, don't you?

The almost perfect wife

Nellie and Dave Warburton were quite the nicest people I ever had the privilege of looking after. Dave worked for John Nisbet who had a small farm a few miles outside Hawick. They lived in one of four cottages on the farm. A shepherd lived in another, a stockman in a third, and the fourth lay unoccupied; it was kept for emergencies and busy times when extra help was required. They had only one son, Rob, who was already twenty when I arrived and was away at agricultural college.

Shortly after I'd started, Dave came to see me; he was accompanied by his wife. "You don't mind if I sit in, do you, Doctor?" she said.

"No, of course not,", I said, though to be honest I usually found it better when they didn't! But I didn't know Nellie in those days.

"I've been getting a bit of chest pain when I exert myself, Doctor, and I thought I should get a check-up." And that was the start of an association, no, a friendship between me and Dave and Nellie. I must say that Nellie never uttered a word during the entire consultation. She just sat with a slight soft smile and before they left shook my hand and said, 'Thank you, Doctor'.

You would think that angina and farm work would make uneasy bed fellows, but the fact is Dave hardly had a day off during the next twenty years! I should mention that a heart bypass was not a possibility in those early days.

After he retired, he asked me if it would be worth his while seeing the cardiologist. "Well, I wouldn't be inconveniencing Mr Nisbet if I had anything done, would I?"

"No, Dave, you wouldn't," I said shaking my head. I don't think Mr Nisbet ever had a more faithful worker. I was delighted when Dave was told after he retired that he could stay in his cottage for as long as he wanted.

Dave duly saw the cardiologist, had a bypass operation and, six weeks later, declared he had never felt so fit. I am sure if it had not been for his wife Nellie, he would never have managed the work he did on the farm. She watched his weight, his diet, his medication, his workload and his rest; nobody but nobody was allowed to take advantage of him. Nellie was the kindest, wisest wife a man could have. As a couple they were just wonderful. Why do I tell you all this? Read on.

Dave had been retired about fifteen years and was about eighty when he died. Nellie phoned me one morning at three o'clock. "Doctor, it's Nellie. Dave has died."

"Oh, Nellie, no. I'll come at once."

"No, Doctor, I don't think you can do anything; the morning will do."

"No, no, I'll come now. I'll be with you in ten minutes."

I pulled on a sweater and a pair of trousers over my pyjamas. My wife murmured, "Are you going out?"

"Yes, Dave Warburton's died."

"Oh no, how awful!"

I hurried downstairs and out to the car.

When I arrived at the cottage I found Nellie sitting in front of the kitchen range next to Dave who was in a chair.

"What exactly happened?" I asked, pulling up a chair and sitting down beside Nellie.

"Well, I got up to go to bed about nine, but Dave said he had a bit of indigestion and he would sit up for a bit and in any case, he wanted to watch a programme on TV on sheep dog trials. I woke about three o'clock and realised he hadn't come to bed, so I came down stairs and found him here."

I took my stethoscope out and listened to his chest and then checked his pupils. I knew he was dead, but I felt I had to go through the motions – well I couldn't do nothing. "Yes, Nellie, you're quite right, Dave is dead." Would 'passed away' have been better? Personally, I've never thought so, but I realise that many people can't or won't use the word 'dead' or 'died'. I wonder, do they find it too final? It's not right or wrong, you just have to use the words that you find best.

Nellie began to cry, not loudly, but quietly sobbing into her shawl and rocking back and forwards. I put my arm round her shoulders. I didn't speak, there didn't seem anything to say. After a few minutes she looked up. "He was a good man; he deserved better."

"Nonsense," I said. "You couldn't have been a better wife, or nursemaid for that matter."

Nellie sighed. "You don't know the half of it, Doctor." I waited, not sure whether to pacify or encourage her. She took out a hankie from her sewing bag, wiped her eyes, blew her nose, and looked up at me. "I'd better tell you, Doctor, I have to tell someone and there really isn't anyone else to tell."

"There's always Rob," I said, "you could tell him if you'd rather."

"Oh no, not Rob, never Rob," and she began to cry again.

I picked up the kettle from the range and made a pot of tea. She took the cup between both her hands and sipped it tentatively.

"It's all so long ago." She wiped her eyes. "The longer I kept it to myself the worse it became, and the more difficult it was to tell anyone. When Dave and I got married, a way back in 1940, the war had just started. Our honeymoon lasted forty-eight hours then he was called up. I didn't see him for four years. That weekend was the first time I had been with a man; you know what I mean. It was not like it is today."

What a hell of a start to a marriage, I thought: she a bonnie lassie and he a fine strapping young man, both desperate for each other and both denied.

"How on earth did you manage?"

"Oh, I wrote to him every week."

"And did he write to you?"

"No, never, Dave couldn't write. A friendly sergeant used to write occasionally but they weren't Dave's letters. It wasn't the same. It was awful... awful." She sat still for a moment then, gathering herself together, started again. "I lived with my father in this cottage; my mother had died when I was born. I helped on the farm. It was hard work – milking cows, singling turnips, stooking the corn then leading it in. There weren't any combines in those days. Time passed quickly, and I suppose things got easier. The following year a German prisoner of war, a student I think, was billeted on the farm to help. We simply knew him as Karl. He was a fine-looking young man, six feet tall, fair haired of course, and when he stripped in the field you couldn't help but admire his muscular chest. He had a funny habit of pulling at his left ear, and at close quarters I noticed the lobe was cleft in two. I think he fiddled with it in an effort to hide it. I asked him once how it had happened and he said he had been born with it. Sometimes he would catch me looking at him and he would smile. He made me feel uncomfortable and I would look away quickly. He didn't say much and kept to himself but in time he really became one of us; everybody liked him, you couldn't help it. Even my father liked him, but I didn't; I loved him. Of course, I

69

never told him and I avoided him as much as possible, but he knew, oh yes, he knew.

"One day a few weeks before the war ended Mr Nisbet received word that Karl would be 'collected' in forty-eight hours by the Military Police and taken back to a camp in Edinburgh, I think. I was heart-broken. That night he tapped on my bedroom window and I let him in. We didn't speak; we just made love. Real love, Doctor, not sex, real love. Afterwards we lay in each other's arms, afraid to sleep, dreading the coming of the morning. The light was just beginning to creep between the curtains when Karl finally rose. He looked at me, held my cheeks between his hands and kissed me gently. His tears mingled with mine. We hugged each other tight then he turned and quietly left. I never saw him again.

"Dave came home about a fortnight later. We settled down to married life. He was good to me and I know he loved me. I was fond of him too. We were both delighted when Rob was born the following spring. We never had any more. It wasn't for want of trying; it just seemed it was not to be. I never told Dave about Karl, Doctor. I wasn't wrong, was I?"

I put down my mug of tea, cold and untouched, and knelt beside Nellie. I hugged her so that she couldn't see my tears. "No Nellie, not wrong, just human. Of course you were right not to tell Dave, be at peace." I felt like a parish priest giving absolution. But what else could I say? Wouldn't I have done the same as Nellie if I had been in her shoes?

"Thank you for coming, Doctor, I'll be all right now. You go home." I hugged her again.

"I'll look back up tomorrow." I stood up, put some peat on the fire, tucked a rug round her knees and left.

As I drove home something Nellie had said kept bothering me 'Karl kept fiddling with his ear'. I had never met Karl and I'd never even seen a picture of him, indeed I don't suppose there was one. I had however seen a cleft ear lobe once before – Rob had one.

The patient, the lawyer, the doctor, and of course, the nurse

"Doctor, do you know a good lawyer?" was hardly the sentence I expected to be greeted with when I paid my usual fortnightly visit to Agnes Barclay-Smith.

"Ye-s," I said in a slightly guarded way, wondering what was coming next.

"Oh good, would you be kind enough to ask him to come and see me."

It wasn't really a question, more of a command; Agnes was a bit like that.

"Don't you think, if I give you his name and address, it would be better if you wrote to him?" I replied, not really wanting to become involved.

"No. I'll tell you why not. You and Nurse have been so good to me that I want to alter my will. I want you to have a chat with the lawyer before I meet him so that you can tell him how I came to be your patient and what Nurse and you have done for me over the last six months. Then you can bring him here and all he will need to do is carry out my instructions. I don't want to waste time having to go through all the reasons for my wishes; you know what lawyers charge."

I smiled to myself and changed the subject. "Well how are you anyway?"

"Great," she replied, "the ulcer on my heel is nearly better now and I tried half a flight of stairs. I'll bet you never thought I would have done that when you saw me six months ago."

"True, you've done well and so has Nurse. Did she tell you she is retiring at the end of the month? I'll miss her."

"Yes, she did. Apparently her husband is retiring too and they are going out to New Zealand to stay with their daughter for a month or so. Have you time for a coffee, Doctor?"

"No, you're kind but I've a lassie in the maternity home who's in labour and I must pop round and see how she's progressing. You be sensible and don't overdo the stairs. Bye, I'll be back in a couple of weeks."

I trotted down the four flights of stairs two at a time; it was harder than going up two at a time, but helped to keep me fit. I was hoping to do a half marathon in a couple of months and the idea of giving up halfway round or coming in last did not appeal.

She's a funny old girl, Agnes, I thought as I drove off. She had been in a private and expensive nursing home in Edinburgh but had rather fallen out with the matron. The only relative she appeared to have was a niece who lived in the Borders and, to cut a long story short, Agnes was removed from the nursing home and came to live with her niece. As the niece was a patient

73

of mine it seemed natural that Agnes should join my list. I was appalled at the state she was in: she had two nasty ulcerated bed sores, one on her bottom and one on her right heel. However there was a snag: Agnes wanted to be a private patient and I didn't take private patients. I remember very clearly saying to her at our first meeting, "I'm sorry, Miss Barclay-Smith, I don't take private patients."

"Why not?" she challenged, "I am very happy to pay your fee. What do you charge?"

"That's not the point. You won't get better treatment than if you are a patient under the NHS; in fact probably worse. If I worry about charging you every time I visit you, then I won't visit you as often as if you were an ordinary patient. You are going to need a lot of visiting until we get you right and I will pop in when I'm passing, whereas if you were private I would tend to limit my visits as much as possible as I don't like charging. Sorry but that's the way I am, if you want private treatment you will have to go elsewhere because my partners think the same as me."

"Wow, you don't beat about the bush, do you?" she replied. "Still I understand where you are coming from. Will you be kind enough to take me on as an NHS patient? But be warned, I've never been one before, so I might misbehave?" She smiled impishly.

"Yes, of course." We shook hands.

And that is how we met. Medically she required a lot of attention both from me and the district nurse,

Helen Welch. Apart from the sores, she was significantly anaemic and under nourished. Over the next few weeks she was seen frequently by both Helen and me; gradually she improved and the nurse did a wonderful job with the sores. Eventually they were all almost totally healed, her blood tests returned to normal, and she had gained a couple of stone.

As I drove home I mulled over Agnes's request for a lawyer.

While I would love a present, I felt uneasy about involving lawyers and wills. I decided to discuss it with my wife. "Hello, darling, is that you?" shouted my wife from the kitchen as I opened the front door.

"Yes. I hope you don't call anyone else darling."

"Oh, I thought it was the postie," she replied provocatively. Lunch will be ready in a couple of minutes; just soup and cheese, big meal tonight," so saying she kissed me and, smiling affectionately, returned to the kitchen.

"Mm, the soup is good. Did you make it?"

"Yes, with the mushrooms we picked on Sunday."

"Darling I've got a problem. I need your advice."

"I hope it's not medical," she replied reluctantly, "I'm getting a bit rusty."

I should mention that my wife was also a doctor; we actually went through six years of medical school together. "No, no, much more difficult. You know Agnes, the nice old lady you had tea with last week?"

"Yes."

"She has put me in a bit of an awkward situation. She has asked me to get a lawyer for her."

"Well what's difficult about that? Get David Robson."

"No, just hear me out. The reason is, she wants to alter her will because Nurse and I have been so good to her and I think she wants to give us something."

"Great, what's wrong with that? What do you think she wants to give you?"

"That's not the point. The point is I don't mind getting something, but I don't want to seem to be part of some conspiracy. Don't you see what I mean?"

"Yes, I do, but I really wouldn't worry about it; lots of doctors get gifts from patients. You gave Charlie a lovely cashmere sweater when our son was born."

I settled down to my lunch and thought no more about it, well not until I went to bed. Feeling less guilty now, I even began to wonder what I might receive or rather how much. No, I mustn't think like that; it's wrong. I know what I'll do; I'll pretend I forgot to contact the lawyer and maybe she will not mention it again. So I turned over and with a clear conscience fell fast asleep.

About two weeks later I dropped in to see Agnes. "Morning, Agnes, I hear from Nurse your sore has finally healed. I want to take another blood sample and if it's normal we can almost sign you off."

"Oh, I hope not, Peter, I enjoy your visits. By the way have you seen the lawyer?"

"No not yet, I've been pretty busy with the measles epidemic but I haven't forgotten. Now if you can pull your sleeve up I will take off some blood; I must say you do have good veins."

"I think one of your ancestors must have been a vampire. You do seem to enjoy taking blood. You do it very well. Is it as easy as it looks?"

"Yes, but I sometimes make a mess of it, especially with fat people when it can be very difficult to find a vein." I inserted the needle and drew off the blood sample. "Fine. Now bend up your arm." I put the blood from the syringe into the small laboratory vial and put a plaster on the punctured vein. "Forgive me but I must fly; see you in a few weeks' time. I'll let you know about the blood test when I receive the results in a few days' time. Bye."

"Now you won't forget about the lawyer will you?" she added as I was leaving.

"Of course not!" I replied over my shoulder as I shut the door.

I realised then, that I couldn't procrastinate any longer. I decided to ring the lawyer that evening.

"Evening, David, Peter here. I hope you're not eating."

"No, haven't started yet. What can I do for you?"

"I'm sorry to ring you at home, but it's rather a delicate matter."

"No problem, not too personal I hope," David replied.

"Well it is in a way. I have a patient who has told me she wants to change her will."

David seemed unconcerned. "That's no problem, perfectly legal; what's the worry?"

"She keeps on saying how kind Nurse and I have been to her and in the same breath says, 'I want to change my will'."

"Excellent," replied David, "what do you want me to do?"

"She wants me to bring you to meet her. Will you?"

"Of course, when?"

"Would tomorrow afternoon suit you or Thursday or Friday? There is really no hurry."

"Thursday would suit me fine. I think we should go separately; after all we are not in cahoots," he jokingly added. "Where does she live?"

"Seventeen Teviot Road. Let's say three p.m. Thanks, David, I am much obliged."

And so it was, at three p.m. the following Thursday Agnes Barclay-Smith, David Robson and yours truly met in Agnes's sitting room. I have to confess that by now my conscience felt clear and I had begun to think of what I might be going to receive, albeit in due course. The idea of a new set of golf clubs, or changing my old split-cane salmon rod for a Sage, which I had been told by those that knew far more about fishing than I did, that it was the Rolls Royce of salmon rods, or if I was really fortunate, maybe even a new car.

I was brought back to earth by Agnes coughing. "Sorry, just a tickle," she reassured me. "Let's all have a cup of tea and then we can get down to business. Peter will you be mother and pour the tea, please?"

I duly did the needful, meanwhile we all discussed the impending General Election. We all agreed that Alec Douglas-Home would be preferable to Harold Wilson. Agnes became quite agitated. "Alec is such a nice man and has much better manners than Wilson and dresses so nicely. Can't stand Wilson." A general murmur of agreement filled the room. Agnes then turned to David. "Now, Mr Robson, I am sure you are a busy man, so I would now like to deal with the matter of my will."

"Certainly," he replied, and taking a sheet of notepaper from his briefcase and a pen from his inside jacket pocket, looked up expectantly. "I assume you already have a will with some other legal firm. May I have their details so as I can contact them?"

"Yes, of course. I have written all the details down here and have a copy of my old will for you. However, I would just like to explain why I want to change it. I have been very ill this last year, but it wasn't until I came under Doctor Neville and Nurse Welch's care, that I got better." At this point I rose from my chair and said that I felt I need not be present for the actual details of the will and moved briefly to look out of the window before turning towards the door.

79

"Oh, no, you must stay, Peter. It's vital, isn't it Mr Robson?"

"Well not really," replied David, "if Peter feels more comfortable leaving the room, we can easily manage without him."

"On no we can't," interjected Agnes, becoming quite worked up. "This is the whole point of him being here. He has been so good to me and I can trust him completely, that's why I want him here today."

"I'm sorry, Agnes," I said, "but I really don't see why I need to be here to discuss your will."

"No, I must say I don't either," said David.

"But he must," said Agnes, "you see he and Nurse have been so kind to me and I want to leave Nurse five hundred pounds."

"All right," said David, "and what about Peter?"

"Oh," said Agnes, turning towards me and smiling affectionately, "I want him to witness this."

"I see," said David, "that's why you wanted Peter here?"

"Yes, he is so trustworthy and such a good friend, I couldn't think of a better person to witness the change I am asking you to make to my will."

I smiled weakly, my dreams of new golf clubs and other possibilities gone for ever. I rose from my chair as did David. We both shook hands with Agnes and left.

"Well, that was a bit of a disappointment for you Peter," remarked David as we walked down the stairway.

"Yes, I must admit it was, but to be fair Nurse did a lot more for her than I did."

"I wouldn't know about that," said David as he opened his car door, "but I'll tell you this, if Nurse gets five hundred pounds, bet she'll think you'll be getting several thousand!"

"And to be truthful," I replied, "I did too."

Follow me

As I mentioned once before I don't like being called out at night; I don't suppose anyone does, but you have to be careful because the temptation is to find an excuse that allows you to stay in bed. 'Won't it wait till the morning?' or 'Take some paracetamol' or perhaps the most dangerous response of all, is making a diagnosis and saying: 'It sounds like flu or (if it's tummy pains) 'it's something you've eaten'. By and large a phone call in the night means *go*. Here is one call you might find interesting.

One night at about one o'clock in the morning, I was awoken from a deep sleep by my phone ringing on and on and on. "Doctor Neville?"

"Yes."

"This is Sergeant Forbes speaking from Melrose Police Station, I have a patient of yours here who requests your presence."

"Melrose is out of my area, so please phone a local doctor."

"Oh no, Doctor, let me explain."

"Don't bother, I don't see people in Melrose. Goodnight."

But before I could put the phone down, he quickly replied, "Doctor, this is a patient of yours and he tells me he is also a very close friend."

"Oh really, who is it?"

He then to my surprise and dismay named the said person. "Oh well, I had better speak to him."

"I'm afraid you can't. He is resting in a cell at the moment. He has been arrested on suspicion of being under the influence of alcohol whilst in charge of a motor vehicle. He has been seen by a local doctor who is of the opinion that he is indeed under the influence of alcohol. Your patient disagrees with the local doctor and requests your help. Or should I say opinion?"

"But I can't see how my opinion is going to make any difference: it would take me at least half an hour to come over, and if I said he was sober it would not contradict the opinion of a doctor who had examined him half an hour earlier. Do you see what I mean?"

"That would not be for me to say. All I know is, he has requested your presence. Will I tell him you are refusing to come?"

By now I was wide awake. "No, I suppose I'll have to; I will be with you in half an hour."

"Thank you, Doctor. Sergeant Milne will be here as I am going home to bed, goodnight."

I pulled on a pair of trousers over my pyjamas, a pair of socks and shoes and finally a thick sweater that a kind patient had knitted for me ('Well you never know when you might have to go out at night') and hurried down stairs. I collected my doctor's bag and set off – the time was twenty past one. I reached Melrose at eight minutes to two and recorded the time in my diary.

"Doctor Neville, it's good to see you again," said a heavily built policeman with a smile. I remembered him well from when he was stationed in Hawick.

"And you, Andrew. How's the family?"

"Fine thank you, sorry to drag you out." The pleasantries over, I was led through to where my 'friendly patient' was waiting.

"So sorry to get you out of bed, Peter, but it's not entirely my fault. They insisted that I should have a second doctor!"

Sergeant Milne interrupted him. "That's not correct. You were merely advised that you could have a second doctor: one of your choice."

"Well now that I am here would you please leave the room Andrew, whilst I examine my patient." The sergeant turned and left the room, shutting the cell door behind him. "Now Will, for god's sake what the hell is going on." I took out my pen and a sheet of notepaper from my bag, made a note of the date and the time; it was 1.58 a.m.

"It's a long story but I'll be as brief as possible. I had been to a rugby dinner which was held in St Boswells. It was well attended and we had some very good speakers but it did drag on a bit and didn't finish until near midnight. I had a fair bit to drink but certainly was not drunk and I reckoned I was fit to drive. After all, as you are supposed to eliminate a unit an hour and the dinner had lasted four hours, I felt reasonably confident that I was fit to drive.

"I took the side road to Lilliesleaf rather than going the long way round by the A68. You know the narrow bridge short of Lilliesleaf, well, I misjudged my line and scraped the left side of the car on the near side of that bridge and then overcompensated and proceeded to scrape the offside, not badly but it was, to say the least, unfortunate. At that moment a car behind me, which I had not noticed, flashed me several times, so I drew into the side of the road and got out of the car. The driver of the car behind also got out of his car and came towards me. 'What on earth do you think you are doing?' he said.

"I realised he was someone I had spoken to, albeit briefly at the dinner.

"'I just made a slight error as I came onto the bridge. I don't think there is much damage,' I said.

"'That is neither here nor there, the fact is you are not fit to be driving. I am attached to the Borders Police Force. The fact that I'm off duty makes no difference; I am obliged to report this to the station in Melrose and require you to come there with me now.'

"'I don't know where the police station is,' I replied.

"'Well you can't leave the car here,' he said, 'it's blocking half the road, just follow me.' And so saying, he returned to his car and drove off. I followed him down to the station. I was then charged with being drunk in charge, which I thought was ridiculous. They then asked me to supply a specimen of urine, which I easily did and was then examined by a GP from Melrose. He gave me a few easy tests which I had no difficulty doing; though I have never been very good at standing on one leg, have you?"

"No. Go on."

"Well there's not much more to say. I must admit I was getting a bit worried and had visions of spending a night behind bars. When they said I could get a doctor of my own I immediately thought of you. I'm sorry, Peter."

"Okay, forget it, but I had better examine you, though as I explained to the sergeant on the phone it is really a waste of time because so much time has passed since the other doctor examined you that whatever I say will have little or no relevance."

I then proceeded to do the standard examination to determine as best I could whether he was fit to drive or not.

"Well, Peter, am I drunk?"

"No, you are not drunk."

"There, I told you so and of more importance I told them so too."

"Hang on, Will, it's not as simple as that. As I have just told you it doesn't mean you were sober when the police doctor examined you at half past midnight or whatever time it was."

"Yes, I follow that. What do you suggest I do?"

"I'll speak to Sergeant Milne, whom I happen to know well from his time when he was a police constable in Hawick, and I will suggest to him that I run you home now and you can arrange for the car to be collected in the morning."

"Perfect, you're a star."

When we finally reached Hawick the town hall clock was standing at 03.10. I dropped Will at his house and finally slipped back into my bed at 03.20 a.m., and I wasn't supposed to be on duty that night! I had felt it was necessary to record all the times accurately. I knew when Will's case came to court, as it was bound to, I would be called as a witness for the defence.

Will phoned me in the morning and was effusive in his thanks and full of apologies. "Peter, you will send me a fee, won't you? I don't expect you can charge the NHS!"

"No, I won't, and no I certainly can't charge the NHS, but you can take me out for dinner after the trial."

"You really think it will come to that?" Will said anxiously.

"What, a trial or a dinner?"

"No! No, of course I'll take you out for dinner whether I win or lose, but you really think it will come to court?"

"Bound to, because the doctor who saw you before me said you were drunk."

"Yes, I suppose so," Will sighed.

Three months later the trial took place. I was called as a witness as expected but realised I was going to be of little help to my friend unless a ploy I had up my sleeve worked. I had discovered, whilst reading an article in a pharmacology journal, a very interesting piece of information regarding the testing of urine for the presence of alcohol. Apparently it had been discovered that if the urine was kept for more than forty-eight hours before being tested the result could be higher than if it were tested within forty-eight hours; something to do with fermentation, I think, but I didn't quite understand the finer points of the article. Now I had been given sight of the laboratory report and noticed it was dated for the Tuesday after the Saturday when the dinner was held. The sample could only have been posted to the lab on the Monday so couldn't have reached there sooner than the Tuesday. It couldn't therefore have been tested within forty-eight hours of being provided by Will. If therefore it was used as the main plank of the prosecution's case against Will, it could be shown to be inaccurate and he would have to be found not guilty. QED (Quod erat demonstrandum). I was really quite excited and felt a bit like Raymond Burr who appeared weekly at that time in a detective series on TV.

I discussed my plan with Will's lawyer and it was agreed that I would bring it up if I was questioned about the urine sample and if I wasn't, he would. After about an hour I was called and sworn in. When I saw who the fiscal (the public prosecutor in Scottish courts) was my heart sank; I had crossed swords with him before, and lost.

His first question was typical of him. "I think the defendant is a friend of yours, is he not?"

"Yes."

"A good friend of many years and also a patient?"

"Yes."

"That must make it difficult for you in a case like this?"

"No."

"Really, I would have thought it would be difficult to find a friend to be drunk and know that you would almost certainly be partially responsible for causing him to lose his licence. However in this case I gather you said he wasn't under the influence of alcohol. Am I correct?"

"Yes."

"Exactly the opposite of Doctor Clark's opinion, who I think I'm right in saying was not a personal friend."

"Objection," said Will's council jumping to his feet, "the fiscal is suggesting that Doctor Neville is biased in his evidence."

"Objection sustained."

"I think you had to drive from Hawick to Melrose to examine your friend. That would take a while?"

"Yes about forty minutes."

"Have you any idea what the time was when you finally examined your patient?"

"Yes, it was 01.58 a.m."

"And how long did it take you?"

"About half an hour."

"And do you know when Doctor Clark examined your friend?"

"Yes I was told it was half past midnight."

"Indeed, so one hour and a half before you. So, the fact that you were a whole hour and a half after Doctor Clark it is not surprising you came to a different conclusion, is it?"

"No."

"Thank you, Doctor, no further questions."

"Thank you, Doctor," said the sheriff, "we need not detain you any longer. I am sure you will wish to return to your practice. Thank you for attending."

"Thank you, my lord." And nodding to the sheriff, I left the witness box and the court. I would have liked to have stayed to hear the outcome, but the sheriff was right I had a lot of work waiting for me back at the surgery.

I found it difficult to concentrate; my mind was on the outcome of the case. Of course I knew Will would be found guilty; the question was what was his punishment to be? I knew he would not go to jail, but to lose his licence would be disastrous as his wife, surprisingly, didn't drive; she had once but following a nasty accident had never got behind the wheel again. A substantial fine would be preferable but whether the defence could persuade the sheriff to adopt that line was impossible to predict. I finished evening surgery and was busy writing some insurance reports when my phone rang.

"Hello, Doctor Neville speaking."

"Hello, Peter, Will here. You'll never guess what happened."

"Tell me."

"I got off. No jail, no fine, nothing."

"Go on, what exactly happened, was it the urine sample being out of date?"

"No, it wasn't even mentioned. After you left I was given a grilling by the fiscal and thought my chance of getting off was miniscule at best. Then the officer, who turned out to be a superintendent, who was in the car behind me when I hit the bridge, was called. You should have been there; the sheriff was magnificent. The fiscal asked the superintendent to go over the details of the accident. The superintendent said he had been following me for about half a mile and actually saw me hit the bridge and so he flashed me. He went on to say we both got out of our cars and he decided I was drunk and explained that my car was blocking the road and told me I couldn't leave it there. This, combined with the fact that I didn't know where in Melrose the police station was, he thought the best thing to do was for me to follow him down to the station.

"At this the sheriff nearly exploded – you should have seen him. 'You what?' he almost shouted. 'You told a man you considered unfit to drive because of alcohol to get into his car and drive behind you to the police station. Superintendent, were you mad?' The superintendent was mortified and mumbled something, but I couldn't hear because of the noise in the court as everybody seemed to be talking to each other. The clerk called for order and when we had all recovered, except for the superintendent who looked shattered, the sheriff said... oh I wish you'd been there. No, the sheriff didn't say that, he said, 'this case should never have come to court'. And then told me I was not guilty and free to leave. I can't tell you how relieved I was."

"I'm delighted to hear that. I do wish I had stayed; I must admit I thought you would probably lose your licence."

"I've booked a table for four, Peter, at Wolfelee for next Friday. I hope that suits?"

"Yes, should be a great evening."

"Oh, one other thing. I've booked a taxi, thought it sensible!"

My big mistake

Looking back on it all now it doesn't seem so bad, but at the time it was a real nightmare. I had retired from general practice at the age of sixty. I had intended to keep going till sixty-five but changed my mind. The advent of Fund Holding was altering how practices were to be run and the nights and weekends on duty seemed to have become more onerous. Nowadays the GPs don't do nights or weekends but I think work harder than we did during the day. If one was on duty at night (after a full eleven-hour day's work), you knew you would be called out, usually between eleven p.m. and three a.m., and probably twice. Am I trying to justify my decision to retire? Yes, I probably am. For a while I was fine and began to play more golf, tidied up the garden and even painted the greenhouse but somehow I felt unfulfilled – something was missing. I suppose I knew all along but a full spring and summer passed before I acknowledged what it was. Of course, I was missing the patients I had known for so long, missing hearing about their joys and, yes, in a funny way, their sorrows and problems too, missing the visits to their homes, but most of all I missed being wanted.

I began to take an interest in the *British Medical Journal* which arrived each week. For months they had remained unopened and unread, still, I'm ashamed to say, in their plastic wrapping, stacked in neat piles in my study, before eventually being moved and stacked in neat piles in the attic.

Well, one day I might need them I told myself in a half-hearted attempt to pacify my guilty feelings. It wasn't so much the articles that interested me now, it was the 'Situations Vacant'. What profession ever offered such a variety of opportunities? Vacancies for general surgeons, orthopaedic surgeons, heart surgeons, anaesthetists, physicians, medical officers of health, general practitioners – there were as many kinds of doctors as recipes for chutney. I fantasised briefly about a job offering three months in the Caribbean as a ship's doctor on a cruise liner. Or should I apply for the post of 'Doctor wanted to accompany ten outdoor enthusiasts white water rafting on the Zambezi'? or, and this one really excited me, 'Doctor wanted for winter season in Val d'Isère'. Why not? I thought. I wanted to try skiing again. I wasn't too old to enjoy a little disco dancing in the evening with the tourists or the chalet girls. Yes, maybe I could even manage a little more than disco dancing with them. I smiled to myself and lent back in my chair. I came back to earth with a bang.

"I've told you not to tilt your chair," my wife said from behind her crossword. "Surrender, two words, four and two."

"Give in," I said. I picked myself up from the floor. Yes, I might just follow up that ad.

I did in fact write for more details, but was too late; the job had been filled a month previously. I checked the date of the BMJ and realised I was six weeks behind in my reading. I promptly discarded the whole of October and opened the newest one dated the 3rd November 1993, and that was the biggest mistake I ever made.

Wanted, Locum Practitioner in single handed Highland Practice, for two weeks in January. I read on avidly. Yes, yes, this would suit me fine. *Applications to the following address or fax or e-mail.* Even better I thought as I hurried upstairs to the computer my children had given to me on my retirement.

"You need one, Dad. Nobody can survive without one nowadays."

Well I could, and still did for that matter. I had battled with the instruction manual but had found it incomprehensible. Just like the MFI instruction manuals for building a chest of drawers. I always ended up with spare pieces left over and drawers that didn't fit. However I had managed to conquer e-mail, and blessing the children's far-sighted kindness, I applied to Doctor Black for further details.

For the next two days I barely left the house and went to my inbox with the urgency of a teenager waiting for the post on Valentine's Day. On the third day the answer came. And so it was that two months later I found myself in Caroldale, a small village about thirty miles northwest of Inverness. My wife, whilst not enthusiastic about me returning to work, was remarkably understanding. "Well, if it stops you being so restless, it might be a good idea," she said. I was pleased that she was happy once again to adopt the role of housekeeper, telephonist, counsellor and adviser (all unpaid). "After all," she said, "I have been doing it for thirty-five years and probably know more than the average young doctor."

It all started well and, as is so often the case in general practice, there was no warning of the nightmare that was about to occur. The first two days had passed without a problem. I was surprised at how easily I had fallen back into the old routine. As I didn't know the patients, they all seemed delightful. Surgeries were much quieter than those I had been used to and there were few requests for house visits. The afternoon was spent in a leisurely fashion motoring up some narrow road through the glorious Highland countryside that I had loved ever since my childhood. It was the third evening just after I had gone to bed that it all began to go wrong. The phone rang.

"Doctor, it's Mabel. Grandpa's not well, will you come at once?"

"Just a minute," I said. "Doctor Black is on holiday. This is Doctor Neville speaking. What's the problem?"

"It's my grandfather, Doctor. He has a bad pain in his tummy; he didn't want me to phone but I know he's not well."

"Can't it wait till the morning?"

"Oh no. You will come, Doctor, won't you?"

"Yes, of course, but tell me your grandfather's name and address please."

"Oh, how silly of me. It's Sutherland, William Sutherland and it's number three Ben More Road."

I had forgotten how much I disliked getting out of bed and for the first time wondered at my decision to go back to work. I dressed quickly. "Won't be long, dear," and, picking up my bag, went downstairs. With some difficulty I found the house. It was a newly built bungalow in the outskirts of the village. There were five or six in the row, none had a name or number that I could see, but there were lights on at one and I parked outside it. An agitated young woman in her twenties appeared at the door as I walked up the path. Before I could say 'hello' she began to speak.

"It's Grandpa, Doctor. You see Mum and Dad are away celebrating their silver wedding and Grandpa has refused to get out of bed for two days. He won't eat anything and he is hardly drinking. I thought he had taken the pet because he had been left behind, but it's not that. He really is ill, Doctor, really I know he is. I should have phoned you earlier. Oh, Doctor, I hope I'm not too late, but he didn't want you. Well not you, Doctor, he just didn't want any doctor. I've told him you're coming and he just swore at me. It's not like him, Doctor, he never swears. Oh he'll be all right, Doctor, won't he?"

She paused for a breath, I tried to look reassuring, patted her gently on the shoulder and, taking her elbow, said, "I am sure we can do something, let's go and see him."

She led me along a narrow corridor into a small bedroom at the back of the house. William was lying submerged in a heap of pillows. A downy lay in a disorderly fashion across him and his feet stuck out at the bottom. On a chair in the corner sat a young man. "Oh, this is my brother Philip, he lives opposite. He's a part time ambulance driver and knows a lot."

He stood up and we shook hands. I was tempted to ask what he knew a lot about but restrained myself; I found it paid not to argue with such people. "He's burst an ulcer, Doctor," said Philip. I nodded, it seemed a safe manoeuvre. I sat down gently on the side of the bed.

"Well now…" I turned quickly to his daughter. "Sorry I've forgotten his name."

"William, Doctor, William Sutherland."

"Well, William, what's the problem?"

The old man eyed me for a moment before replying. "It's nothing, Doctor, you know these young things are always fussing. Fuss, fuss, fuss. Give me a day or two and I'll be fine." He turned his eyes away and looked at Mabel. "You shouldn't have called the doctor; you know I didn't want him." He shut his eyes and grunted.

That he was in pain there was no doubt. He frowned continuously and his breathing was laboured.

"Well, let's just have a look at you, William. Put out your tongue, please." Grudgingly he did; it was dry and furred like a shoe's insole. His breath smelt strongly of acetone. "Let's have a wee look at your tummy." I knelt on the floor, undid the bottom two buttons of his pyjama jacket and the cord of his trousers. Gently I palpated his tummy, all the time watching his face. Whenever I pressed firmly he winced. "It's sore, isn't it, William?"

"Not much, I've known worse, quite often get it. It'll go away."

"I don't think so this time, William. You've burst your ulcer."

Philip nodded, "I agree, Doctor."

"I'll phone the hospital and arrange for your admission, William; you will need an operation tonight. With a bit of luck you will be back home within a week."

"I won't," he said.

"Of course you will," I replied. "They don't keep patients in long nowadays."

"I won't, 'cos I'm not going in," William said defiantly.

"But you must," I said.

"Yes, Grandpa, you must," said Mabel.

Philip came and lent over the bed. "Come on, Grandpa, be sensible. You know the doctor's right. You'll have to go in and we'll come and visit you, and before you know it you'll be home."

99

"I am not going in – now that's enough. Leave me alone. Thank you, Doctor, but you can go."

"Now, William," I said, becoming as frustrated as Philip and Mabel. "You must go in; you have no choice. If you don't, you'll…" I hesitated.

"I'll what?"

"You'll die," I replied slightly aggressively. Philip nodded. Mabel caught her breath.

"I'm sorry, William," I said, "but that's a fact: if you don't go in you'll die."

He eyed me sadly like a beaten spaniel. "Well so be it. I've had a good life and if that's what's to be, so be it," and pulling his downy up around his shoulders turned with difficulty and faced the wall. Slowly I stood up, shrugged my shoulders and put my stethoscope back in my pocket and signalled to Mabel and Philip to follow me out of the room. We went through to the sitting room and sat down.

"Doctor, you can't just let him die. You must do something," said Mabel.

"That's right. Mabel's right. You must do something," said Philip.

I thought for a moment and cursed that I had ever taken the job. "I am as concerned as you are," I said, "but your grandpa is eighty-six, he's had a long life, and he's made up his mind. If he is going to die he wants to die in his own bed."

"But he's off his head," said Mabel.

"That's right," said Philip. "He's ill. He doesn't know what he's doing."

"I'm afraid he does know what he's doing," I said, "and whether I like it or not, he is perfectly entitled to stay in his bed and if that means he dies, I'm afraid there is nothing you or I can do about it. I'll give him an injection to ease his pain. I'm sorry but that's all that can be done."

"We'll see about that. Doctor Black would never have let him stay here and die." Philip was understandably upset.

I went back to the bedroom. "I would like to give you an injection, William, to ease your pain, and it will help to give you a good night's sleep."

"Thank you, Doctor."

Mabel then saw me to the front door. "I'm sorry," I said again, "I'll look in first thing in the morning on my way to the surgery."

"You needn't bother," said Philip. "We'll get someone else."

Mabel was more polite. "Thank you for coming. Please come back in the morning. Philip doesn't mean what he said; it's just we're so upset."

"I know, I understand. I'll be back."

I turned, walked down the path, climbed into my car and slowly drove away. As I drove home I began to wonder, had I done the right thing? Should I have sent him in against his wishes? Indeed could I have? Should I have certified him insane, as being a danger to himself.

The hospital staff would then have come and removed him, if necessary by force. What if he died during the night, would the family sue me? At worst if they did the Medical and Dental Defence Union would defend me and pay any damages. Then the awful truth struck me. Although I had been a member of the union all my working days I had resigned when I stopped working and had forgotten to join again when I took up the locum post. I felt quite faint and pulled into a passing place. I sat there sweating profusely. I opened the car window and breathed in the cold night air; slowly my head cleared. Oh why, oh why had I ever taken the job. I drove home slowly. I poured myself a large whisky, drank half and took the rest upstairs to bed. I normally never drank when I was on duty but this time I really needed it. The bedroom light was still on and my wife lay sound asleep, snoring quietly, her book balanced precariously across her chest. She woke as I climbed into bed.

"Was it necessary?" she said.

"Oh yes, very."

"Good," she replied and turned on her side and resumed her snoring.

I tossed and turned. I realised whether I was right or wrong I would have a lawsuit on my hands if William Sutherland died. And that is exactly what happened. Why, oh why, hadn't I stuck to painting the greenhouse?

The court was full when I was led into the witness box. The sheriff looked a nice man. He had a benign round red face. He wore a pair of half glasses and a suggestion of a smile; I had a vague feeling I had seen him before but just couldn't place him. He nodded to the assembled lawyers and members of the public as he sat down. He opened the proceedings by stating that this was simply an inquiry into a tragic sudden death and, eyeing me over his glasses, added, "You are not on trial, Doctor Neville, but are here to explain the events that led up to Mr Sutherland's tragic death, so that this court is able to reach a decision as to whether or not further action requires to be taken." He then invited the procurator fiscal to address the court.

I felt slightly reassured. This feeling evaporated quickly when the procurator fiscal stood up. He was a man in his late fifties I reckoned. He was, I thought, surprisingly untidy. He had a short beard and long sideburns. He smiled to the sheriff and gave a half bow. Turning to me his smile was rapidly replaced by what I can only describe as a scowl of what seemed to me to be, wicked malevolence. After establishing my full name and address and qualifications, and one or two seemingly unnecessary facts, he fixed me with what I can only describe as a most unfriendly look. "Tell me, Doctor, is it the case that you took early retirement from your practice?"

"Well, I had been in practice for thirty-five years," I said defensively.

"Yes, yes, but most people don't retire at sixty."

I made no reply.

"Did you find it too hard work?"

"Well, it was a busy practice."

"Yes, but I think most of us would think that early to retire."

He was keeping at me like a terrier with a bone.

"Was it because you felt it was getting too much for you physically?"

"Certainly not. I was physically very fit," I replied getting a bit annoyed. I felt he was trying to trick me in some way.

"So it was more a mental problem, was it?" the fiscal asked provocatively.

"Certainly not," I replied crossly.

The fiscal was now in full stride. "I don't follow you, Doctor. It wasn't physical and it wasn't mental, what was it?"

"What was what?" I replied equally crossly.

"I am trying to establish why you retired so soon. It seems to me," he said raising his voice, "you are reluctant to tell me."

The sheriff intervened. "There is no good getting cross with the doctor. If you don't like his answers, don't ask the questions."

"I put it to you, Doctor," said the fiscal, "that the reason you retired was very understandable, that you had had enough of what had been a very stressful job."

"Yes, well I felt I had done enough and... er... thought it would be nice to take a rest," I added rather feebly.

The sheriff smiled; the fiscal made a cynical grimace. I looked at my feet. I couldn't take much more of this. I was beginning to sweat. "May I have a glass of water?" One was produced at once.

"But in fact you changed your mind, Doctor, didn't you?"

"Yes. I found I missed the work so I took this locum job."

"Yes, rather a cushy job compared with the job you had been used to, and well paid I should think. Were you busy?"

"No."

"You no doubt felt quite relaxed, not too tired, am I right?"

"Yes."

"Let us move on, Doctor, to the telephone call from the Sutherlands. I gather you were in bed at the time. Were you asleep?"

"No."

"But I gather you weren't keen to go?"

"Well that's not quite right," I said defensively.

"I think it is, Doctor. Your exact words were, I believe, 'Can it not wait till the morning.' Is that not true?"

"Yes."

"I don't blame you, Doctor, no one likes getting out of bed at one in the morning, but you were told you had to and so you went?"

"Yes."

"Let us move on to your consultation. You first of all took a history, as you doctors like to call it, from Mr Sutherland and then examined him. Was he cooperative?"

"Yes."

"What happened next?"

"I gave him my opinion as to what was wrong with him and…"

"Let me stop you there. Am I right in saying his grandson Philip and granddaughter Mabel were present during the consultation and they agreed with your opinion?"

"Yes."

"Philip says you spent only ten minutes with his grandfather. Is that so?"

"Well I didn't time myself. I just spent as long as was necessary."

"I see. Enough time to listen, to take his history, examine him, and then discuss what was needed?"

"Yes." I wondered where this was leading.

"Was he co-operative?"

"Yes, but he didn't really want me in the first place." I was getting desperate. I took another sip of water.

"So he took some coaxing, but he didn't stop you from examining him?"

"No."

"What did you find?"

"He had a fever, was dehydrated and had a rigid abdomen. I thought he had a burst ulcer."

"A potentially fatal condition, isn't it, Doctor?"

"Yes."

"So what did you do?"

"I advised him that he needed an operation, but he said he wasn't having one and refused to go to hospital."

"I understand from his granddaughter that you told him he would die if he didn't go to hospital. Is that so?"

"Yes."

"So you left the room and after a brief talk to Mabel and Philip said you would come back in the morning."

"Well I gave Mr Sutherland a pain killing injection first, but there didn't seem anything more to be done."

"You didn't seem to try very hard, Doctor. Do you not think it deserved a little more effort on your part? After all, if he was so ill was he really a good judge of what was best for himself?"

"No."

"And yet you walked away knowing, as you put it, that he would probably die."

I realised that the fiscal was making me out to be an uncaring doctor who just couldn't be bothered, but it wasn't like that. I know it sounded bad, but I really had tried, despite what Philip and Mabel said and if I had to do it again I would do exactly the same. The old man was tired of life. He didn't want to go to some strange hospital, lie in a strange bed and be looked after by people he didn't know. He just wanted to stay in his own home and in his own bed. I thought the sheriff would have understood, after all he wasn't that much younger than me. The fiscal obviously didn't and probably never would. The sheriff took his glasses off. The smile had left his face. The fiscal sat back a supercilious smirk on his face. I felt quite faint. The courtroom began to swim. I sat down. I felt a hand on my shoulder. "Get up. Get up." I opened my eyes.

"Come on, lazy bones, you'll never be in time for the morning surgery."

I stared in disbelief at my wife. Was it all a dreadful dream? I dressed quickly, refused breakfast and hurried off to see William Sutherland. As I turned into their narrow road my heart stopped, for outside number three a hearse was parked. I drew up behind it, jumped out, and strode up the garden path. The front door was open. I knocked and didn't wait.

"It's just me," I shouted.

"Come in, Doctor," Mabel replied. I walked along the narrow corridor. The bedroom door was half open. I couldn't see the bed. I didn't need to; what I could see told me all. Sitting on a chair, his head in his hands, sat Philip. He looked up as I entered and then looked quickly away. I pushed the door further open.

"Morning, Doctor, I'm not dead after all." William Sutherland sat propped up on his pillows beaming broadly.

"Morning, Doctor," said Mabel. "I was sorry to get you out of bed last night. Grandpa seems better this morning. I hope you had a good night?"

I smiled weakly.

"Well, William, let's just check up on you."

I examined his tummy again. It was clear to me that although he might be feeling better the problem was still there.

"Well," he said. "What do you think, Doctor?"

"I'll tell you what I think. I think you've a perforated ulcer. And I'll tell you something else. Last night you did what you wanted to do; today you're doing what I want. You're going in to hospital. Right?"

"Okay, Doctor, if that's what you think, I'll go." The three of us looked at him in amazement. Before he could change his mind, I turned to Philip.

"Where's the phone?"

"Come through to the vestibule, please," and leading me back along the corridor he pointed to the phone which was standing on a small table behind the front door.

"I'm sorry about last night, Doctor. I was rude to you, I shouldn't have been. If you wait a moment I'll just go across to my home and change, then I'll take Grandpa in the ambulance."

"But what's the hearse doing here?" I asked.

"Oh it's mine," said Philip. "I'm just a part-time ambulance man and a part-time undertaker. You see we don't have many deaths here."

Your number please

Away back before computers were commonplace I thought, just maybe, that the practice should be considering whether to install computers or not. All records were, up until the early '90s, handwritten and filed in envelopes. It was obvious that this could not continue. As the envelopes became fatter and fatter something would have to give. I was lucky, for my retirement intervened and saved me from learning about computers, or at least that was what I thought. My ignorance caught up with me, well to be truthful it never left me, and I was confronted with it on a locum I did in the Highlands. I had been asked by a young doctor who was a friend of one of my children if I could do a fortnight's locum. It never occurred to me that he might be 'computerised'. I arrived one Sunday and, after a delicious lunch in his house, Doctor Green suggested we go down to his surgery. It was really just an old shop that he had converted into his practice premises. It had a small reception/waiting room, his consulting room, a large walk-in cupboard where he kept all the medicines (his was a dispensing practice as there was no chemist in the village) and a small toilet.

"Well," he said, "not as grand a place as yours I expect." I saw no point in replying, after all he was in a remote part of Scotland and you couldn't really expect him to be up to date, could you?

"Oh, by the way," he said, "I haven't yet completed my change from written records to computers. I expect you did that years ago. Are you an expert with computers?"

"Oh no, not an expert, no certainly not," I replied. At least I was being honest.

Doctor Green continued talking about his computers. "I have about half the practice on the computer and half still to do, so when someone comes in it's important you ask them if they have a number. Those that have, you just pop it onto the screen and there will be the history and all the relative details of the previous illnesses and present drug regime. I just don't know how I managed before; it is essential for good twentieth-century medicine. Don't you agree?"

At that moment I was literally saved by the bell because his phone rang.

I realised that this was maybe a remote practice but, was more up to date than mine had been.

"Okay, Peter, any questions?"

"No, that's fine." It wasn't, but there was nothing I could do about it and asking questions would only reveal my ignorance, and no one likes doing that, do they?

Monday morning saw me arrive early at the surgery. "Good morning, Doctor," said an attractive girl who couldn't have been much older than my oldest grandchild. "You are early. The first patient isn't due for another hour. We don't actually make appointments before nine a.m. and it's just after eight."

"Yes, I know, but I thought it would give me a chance to get used to various things before anyone arrived."

"Very good idea. I'll bring you a coffee. Milk and sugar?"

"Yes, that would be kind. By the way are you a whiz-kid with computers? I expect you are; I know my grandchildren are."

"I'm not sure about being called a whiz-kid but, yes, I am computer literate. Any problems just buzz through to me; but coming from a big town, I should think it's more likely to be me buzzing you for help."

I smiled rather pathetically and said nothing. I went through to my consulting room and sat down and stared vacantly at the big black screen. I pressed the on button, but nothing happened. Oh my god, I wish to goodness I had admitted at the beginning that I knew nothing about computers, but it was too late now. Mary came in with the coffee.

"Managing okay?" she said with a slight smile.

"I can't seem to turn it on, Mary, seems a different model to mine."

"Oh, it's not plugged in at the wall; we always unplug it at night." She smiled again.

"Of course, how stupid of me," I replied.

113

"Easy done," she said still smiling, and bending down plugged it in.

"Just remind me how you bring up the patient details, please, Mary."

Half an hour later I felt more confident. "Thank you, Mary, I'm a bit rusty or to be perfectly honest I am an absolute beginner with computers." There I'd confessed and immediately felt better. Is that how you get rid of sinning, I wondered, maybe I should change my religion.

"No problem, Doctor, you can't be expected to be computer literate at your age. It's a young person's domain."

"Yes, I think you are absolutely right," I replied slightly pathetically.

I spent the next ten minutes practising by myself. My buzzer went off. "It's your first patient, Doctor, Mrs Hamilton. Will I send her in?"

"Yes, please do."

As she entered, I stood up, introduced myself and apologised that her doctor was away on a well-earned holiday, but I was sure I could help her.

She smiled. "I wonder if I could—"

I held up my hand. "Please, Mrs Hamilton, sorry to interrupt you but have you a number?"

"Yes it's 167 but—"

Again I raised my hand. "Sorry to stop you again but I must just do something," and looking at the screen I typed in 167.

To my surprise and delight up came Esther Hamilton. "Ah, Mrs Hamilton, are you Esther Hamilton?"

"Yes but—"

By now I was well in to my stride and, transfixed by my new toy, I stared in delight at my screen. "Yes, I have it here, Esther Hamilton of 25 Ben More Drive. Is that correct?"

"Yes," she replied, in a rather irritated tone I thought.

"I see you are on digoxin and warfarin and you had a triple bypass in Edinburgh last December. How are you keeping now?" I looked away from the screen for a brief moment. I must say this was a new world for me, quite fascinating.

"Very well, Doctor, but—" I hardly heard her reply.

"I apologise for having to go through your details, but Doctor Green told me to check your number before I started the consultation so that I would know all about you and so avoid making any mistakes. I'm sure you understand." I smiled disarmingly at Mrs Hamilton. "Now tell me, what can I do for you?"

"May I have my husband's pills, please?" And before I could say another word Mrs Hamilton raised her hand. "A moment please, Doctor," then continued, "and he doesn't have a number yet." She sat back, rather triumphantly I thought.

I went to the filing cabinet, retrieved the appropriate file, confirmed what his medication was and obtained the drugs from the drug cupboard and gave them to Mrs Hamilton.

"Thank you, Doctor, have a nice day," and she hurried out of the room. I don't like that expression and I didn't expect to hear it in the Highlands of Scotland. Still I suppose she meant well!

Why Gordon didn't eat his breakfast

I am telling you this tale because it illustrates how people never cease to amaze one in either doing the unexpected, or in this case, saying the unexpected.

I was somewhat surprised when Doctor Black phoned me on a Sunday afternoon in May '97; after all it was only a couple of months or so since I had done a locum for him. "Good evening, Peter," he said in his usual friendly voice. "How's life with you? Well I hope?"

"Fine, thank you."

"Good, good, glad to hear you're well." There was a slight pause. "Not working too hard, I hope." He laughed and didn't wait for an answer. "I was wondering if you were by any chance free next week. I know it's short notice but to be perfectly honest I've been offered a rod on the Helmsdale and I'm told the salmon are on the move and it's not a chance to be missed."

"Next week you say. Well I can understand your keenness to fish the Helmsdale; I did myself once but just for a day. To be honest it was enough; we got devoured by midges. Still they shouldn't be too bad in May. Could I ring you back? I'll need to talk to June."

"Of course, no hurry. Well that's not quite true but it would be great if you could; you went down so well with everybody last time." I smiled to myself remembering my 'big mistake'.

"I'll phone you back this evening."

"You are kind. I look forward to hearing from you."

"Is that who I think it was?" my wife asked.

"Yes, he wants me to do another week's locum."

"When?"

"Next week."

"What, next week? You can't."

"Why not?"

"My sister's coming to stay."

I didn't get on with June's sister. Indeed I often wondered if they came out of the same nest.

"You can put her off for a couple of weeks, can't you?" I said hopefully (thinking, or forever if possible). "Michael's desperate. He says the fish are running on the Helmsdale and he has been offered a rod. If he catches some, we might get one and you know how you like smoked salmon."

"Well, you phone her?" June replied.

"Oh, darling, that's a bit hard. You know she not my best friend."

"Well I'm not phoning her."

"All right, if you won't I suppose I have to."

And that's what I did, using an old excuse that always seemed to work, namely did she mind if my son and his Italian wife were here at the same time?

I duly phoned her and as expected she agreed to delay her visit.

"Well that seems to be fine. She agreed to come later in the month. Does that suit you, darling?"

"Actually, I'm delighted," my wife replied. "I enjoyed our last visit up north and you know I don't find Bessie the easiest of visitors." She smiled sweetly and triumphantly.

I rang Doctor Black and arranged to go up the following Sunday.

It may surprise some of you that I was happy to go back to Caroldale after my previous experience but as the saying goes, all's well that ends well.

I felt more settled this time. I knew my way about the place and received a very friendly welcome from the receptionist in the practice and the district nurse.

"Nice to see you again," they said almost in unison as I walked in the door of the surgery.

"Good to be back," I replied. "What have you got for me today? Nothing too demanding I hope."

"Not sure about that," replied the nurse and proceeded to tell me a long and convoluted story about someone who had sent a request for a home visit.

In fact I had seen the patient on my previous visit as a locum and remembered him well. Let me tell you about him. Gordon Ross was a farmer, well a crofter really. He just had a small acreage and I always wondered how he made a decent living from it, but he seemed to manage; he must have had to work hard. He

119

had three sons which was the problem, for when they were old enough, they found themselves doing all the hard work on the farm. It was then that Gordon developed his 'abdominal pains' which forced him to stay in bed or sit in front of the fire or, when the lamb sales came along, he would put up with pain and struggle to Lairg to sell his lambs. He would spend much of the day in the bar with other farmers. Doctor Black told me that he had seen Gordon many times and done all manner of tests on him, and had referred him to Raigmore, the hospital in Inverness, for a second opinion but nothing was found.

"I'll just have to put up with it, Doctor, won't I?" he said when I last saw him.

"I wonder if you cut out the whisky, Gordon. Do you think that might help?" I suggested.

"Oh, Doctor, I wish I could. I don't like it but it's the only thing that helps the pain." I resisted any answer.

The three boys had finally, one by one, left home, and with them went the stock and Gordon was left with his long-suffering wife Millie and his old age pension.

"All right, I will go after the morning surgery but it will be the usual waste of time," I said slightly reluctantly.

"I think he will have heard that you were here again and he is just taking advantage of you," said the receptionist.

"I don't mind going," I replied, "so long as I'm not busy but as you know it takes about half an hour to get there."

I finished the morning surgery about ten o'clock, had a cup of tea then set off for 'West View'. Well named as the croft had a tremendous view of what my wife once described, after a liquid lunch, as 'miles and miles of bugger all'.

She was right. There really was nothing to see except an endless panorama of heather and bog and wispy grass, watched over by seagulls and curlews. Almost all the time a strong wind blew and there was no shelter. The croft was a single-storey building which seemed to have had several additions, no doubt required as the family grew, but now the place looked forgotten and uncared for. If there had ever been a garden it was long gone. There was little paint round the windows and what was left was holding on by its fingertips. The outer walls, once white, were now largely brown from the water running off the corrugated iron roof. I parked the car and, avoiding as best I could the numerous puddles, reached the front door.

It was ajar and after knocking pushed it open with difficulty; I think the hinge was either broken or needed oil or both.

"It's just me, Millie." Gordon's wife was fast asleep sitting in her rocking chair with her slippered feet resting on an old black cooking range. A kettle purred softly on the hot plate. I coughed loudly but Millie didn't move. I approached the chair and gently began to rock it. Her feet fell of the fender and she sat up with a start.

"Oh it's you, Doctor, I didn't hear you. I think I must have fallen asleep. Thank you for coming." She picked up a stick that lay beside her chair and began to rise.

"Don't move, Millie," I said putting a restraining hand gently on her shoulder.

She sank back with a sigh. "It's Gordon, Doctor, it's those pains again. He'll be glad it's you; he doesn't think Doctor Black is very good. Personally, I don't think anyone can cure his pains. If you ask me it's psychosomatic."

I couldn't resist a smile. "What on earth gave you that idea? Have you been reading those medical books again?" I knew that one of her sons had given her a book for her Christmas entitled *All You Need To Know About Your Body*. "I told you last time I was here you'd be better keeping to *The People's Friend*."

"I am fed up with them; all the stories end happily and you know that as soon as you start them. I'd rather have a bit of mystery. Well I had better not keep you. Gordon will be waiting impatiently for you; he hadn't eaten his breakfast when I last looked in. See if you can do something for him; I'm at the end of my tether. I sometimes wish the good Lord would call him home. Oh dear, is that an awful thing to say? I don't mean to be unkind, Doctor, but honestly he doesn't have much of a life and I am finding everything getting on top of me."

122

"There now don't distress yourself. You've been a wonderful wife to him. I'll go through and see him." I knew from past experience that there would be nothing wrong with him; there never was. I rather agreed with Millie about the good Lord stepping in.

I gave her a reassuring pat on the shoulder and walked through to the bedroom.

There he was, just as he always was when he was expecting the doctor, sitting propped up on his pillows, sound asleep. A breakfast tray lay across his lap, a pot of tea, a boiled egg, some toast and a saucer of butter and a small jar of honey, all untouched. A sliver of sickness dribbled down from the side of his mouth and his skin had a slightly jaundiced look; he didn't look well. I sat on the bed and took his wrist in my hand to check his pulse. He didn't have one. Gordon was dead. I checked his heart with my stethoscope out of habit, but I knew he was dead.

I removed the breakfast tray and pulled the sheet up over his face. I hesitated, trying to think how I would break the news to Millie. Breaking good news is easy, breaking very good news almost a privilege, but breaking bad news is difficult and breaking very bad news is… well there is no easy way. I remember once going to a house to tell a lady that her husband had been killed in an accident at work. When I knocked on her door I was greeted with, "Ah, Doctor, you've just come at the right moment. I've been baking scones you must come in and have one."

How would I break the news to Millie? I stood up and walked slowly through to the kitchen. Millie was still sitting beside the range and was now knitting. She looked up and smiled. "Well how is he, Doctor?" I pulled up a kitchen chair and sat down beside her. She continued knitting. "Has he still got the pains?"

"No…" and before I could complete what I was about to say Millie said, "Oh that's good."

"Well not really, Millie, you see he has no pain because, well he's… dead." That wasn't the way I had intended to break the news, but it just seemed to come out like that. I didn't know what else to say.

"Ah well," said Millie. "that's probably why he didn't eat his breakfast."

You must admit, as I said at the beginning, that what Millie said was not quite what you would have expected.

Jealous love

It was as a result of the war in the Falklands that Hazel and Bill Watson came to settle in our village. He didn't talk much about his experience, but I gathered from his wife that he had nearly drowned when his ship was sunk following a direct hit. He was trapped below deck and it was only by sheer luck that he escaped when the ship's arsenal blew up and he managed to swim to the surface. Apart from significant damage to his hearing and a badly lacerated left thigh he had no serious injuries. He swore he would never go to sea again or work in a confined space. I met him whilst doing an extended locum in the Highlands.

After his discharge from the Navy he enrolled on a game keeping course at the local college of further education. Two years later he applied for, and was successful in, obtaining the post of underkeeper on Vice Admiral Sir William Blair's estate at Carolmore. I learnt all this from Hazel when she came to register with the practice. She had made an appointment to see me for her 'New patient consultation'. She was a slim girl, probably no more than seven and a half stone. The fact that she was about five foot eight inches tall and wore high heels merely added to her thin appearance. A silver belt tied tightly round a neat black dress gave some shape to her body; naked she must have been as straight as a broom handle. Her neck was long too but had a fullness, an overactive thyroid I thought to myself, a view supported by her protruding eyes. She handed me two cards and smiled gently. One was for Hazel Clark Watson and the other was William Horatius Watson.

"Will your husband be coming in sometime?" I asked.

She hesitated, then smiled again but this time an almost anxious frown flitted momentarily across her forehead. "Yes, I think so. He asked me to apologise for not coming with me but he is very busy preparing for the pheasant shoot on Saturday."

"Oh, he's a gamekeeper, is he? Whereabouts?"

"On Carolmore Estate"

"Really, I must look out for him when I shoot there next month. Has he always been a gamekeeper?"

It was then that she told me about his experience in the Falklands War.

"And what about you, any family?" I asked.

"No, not yet."

"Ah well, plenty of time. So there are just the two of you?"

"Yes."

"And what do you do whilst your husband's busy with the pheasants?"

"I've been very fortunate. I have always been interested in animals and I have been lucky enough to get a job with Mr Asher the vet. A sort of jack-of-all-trades, manning the phone, cleaning out the cages and even helping a little sometimes on operating days. Oh nothing grand you know, just holding the dog or cutting the stitches. I love animals and I love the work."

"And your health, tell me about it. Any serious illnesses, or operations?"

"No, well nothing much." Again the nervous smile accompanied by the slight frown clouded her face. I had the impression something was bothering her, but maybe today was not the right time to pursue things.

"Well it's nice to meet you. I'll send for your previous notes and when I get them Hazel, my receptionist, will send you an appointment to come in for a medical."

"Is that really necessary? I'm as fit as a fiddle."

"I'm sure you are but we encourage all new patients to have one."

"But I don't have to, do I?"

"No." I realised I was in danger of upsetting her. "Don't worry about it. It's no big deal." She stood up to leave, and so did I.

"Will you ask your husband, William, to pop in when things quieten down?"

"Oh, it's not William; it's Bill. Yes, I'll tell him. Good to meet you and don't worry about me." So saying, we shook hands and she left.

Her previous health records arrived about six weeks later and made interesting reading. Hazel had lived for the first seventeen years of her life in Lairg and apart from the usual childhood illnesses seemed to have had no major problems. A salmon hook in her left ear when she was fourteen, and a sprained ankle whilst attempting to run from Aviemore through the Lairig Ghru to Braemar at the age of sixteen, suggested a healthy outdoor life.

Her problems started when she was eighteen. She had obviously done well at school and been accepted for Edinburgh University, for her new address was Pollock Halls which I knew from my own student days was where many of the university students stayed. She then became a regular visitor to the student health service practice. Frequent consultations were recorded over the next six months for a variety of what were diagnosed as stress disorders: headaches, loss of weight, no periods again (pregnancy test negative – denies any possibility of pregnancy) and so it went on. Hardly a week seemed to have passed without Hazel seeing one of the practice doctors. Then early in May she took an overdose of aspirin. She was apparently discovered by another student and was rushed to hospital. After a stomach wash out, she was referred to a psychiatrist who diagnosed an 'acute anxiety state' and prescribed Valium. Shortly after that she must have left the university because the next entry on her card showed she was back in Lairg. No further entries occurred during the next five years then in July '89 she was prescribed an oral contraceptive and a note in her card stated that she was moving south and planning to get married.

She didn't come in for her medical despite our requests and I didn't pursue her. I decided, after reading her notes, that she probably didn't have an overactive thyroid, and was thin because she was suffering from a chronic anxiety state and I thought it best to let things be for the moment.

Her husband did come in. He was a big strongly built man. His face bronzed from days in the fresh air, and his ginger hair sprouted in all directions and had it not been for his deer stalker, which he had kept on, I think it would have flown away. He touched it with his fore finger and smiled kindly. "Well, Doc, how are you?"

"Oh fine I think, I never really bother about it."

"What do you want to do to me?" he asked.

"Nothing much, just your height, weight and blood pressure and a quick sounding of your chest."

He took his jacket off and rolled up his sleeve. A large pheasant was tattooed on his left bicep and as he bent his arm it seemed to flutter its wings.

"You like it, Doc?" he asked, seeing me staring at the tattoo.

"Very good, never seen one like it."

"Got it done one night in Cairo when I was pissed. Rather regretted it in the morning. Hazel doesn't like it but I said a bird on the arm's worth two in the bush." He laughed again.

I took his blood pressure. "Fine, and what about your general health, any problems?"

"No, grand, first class, best thing I ever did taking up this gamekeeping business. You can't beat the open air. Don't know how you cope being stuck in here all day listing to a load of moaners."

"How's Hazel?" I asked.

"Not bad, well so-so. She worries a lot."

"What about?"

"Well may you ask, everything and nothing. In fact I wanted her to come and see you but she said she'd been once and saw no point coming again when there was nothing wrong with her."

"How long have you been married?"

For a second he seemed to hesitate, surely he hadn't forgotten already. I glanced up at him, he rubbed his left eye as if there was something irritating it and looked away.

"About four years."

"Everything all right?"

"Not bad, Doc, fine really. Good days and bad days. You know how it is. Well I mustn't blether on. We're busy catching up the hens; the admiral wants us to do our own rearing next year. He stood up, rolled down his sleeve, put on his jacket and briefly touching his cap, opened the surgery door and was gone.

There are three times when I don't like being phoned: when I've just climbed into bed, started my meal, or sat down on the loo. It was on the second occasion some three weeks later at lunch time that I next spoke to Bill. I was eyeing a nice piece of fillet steak when the phone rang.

"You answer please, dear," I said to my wife and she duly obliged.

Covering the mouthpiece, she turned to me. "It's Bill Watson the gamekeeper, he sounds upset."

"Oh blast, all right. Hello, Doctor Neville here."

"Doctor, it's Hazel. She's slashed her wrist; it's bleeding badly. I've tied a tea towel round the cut but it's still oozing through."

"How did it happen?"

"She took my cut-throat and slashed her wrist just after I'd left the house. Fortunately, I had forgotten my car keys and went back in and there she was, blood all over the place."

"Okay, keep pressure on the wound and I'll be with you in ten minutes." I grabbed my bag and as I left the house shouted to my wife to call the ambulance and ask them to go at once to Bill's cottage. When I arrived, Hazel was sitting on a chair by the fire crying. Bill was kneeling beside her holding a cloth over the wound. Blood was splattered around everywhere: the mantelpiece, the hearth, the rug in front of the fire and Hazel's skirt and blouse were covered.

"All right, Hazel," I said, putting an arm round her shoulder. "We'll get you up to the casualty department in the local hospital and have you right as rain in no time."

I applied a firm bandage over the tea towel which stopped the oozing.

"Bill, go with Hazel in the ambulance and I'll go on and get things ready."

I had barely scrubbed up in theatre when Hazel was wheeled in. "Bill, you wait in the out-patient department and I'll see you when I've finished."

Hazel lay on the theatre table, pale and sweating. Her eyes were red from crying, but apart from an occasional sniff she made no sound.

"Well now let's have a look and see what's what," I said reassuringly.

"Sorry, Doctor." she said, "I couldn't help it; I was desperate."

"There now, let's get this sorted and then you and I will have a chat."

The out-patient theatre sister was an experienced and kindly middle-aged woman who had seen it all before. She held Hazel's other hand and wiped the sweat gently from her brow. Slowly I loosened the bandage and then the tea towel, and at the same time I kept pressure just above the wound. A clean cut about one and a half inches wide stretched across the front of her wrist.

"Let me see you move your fingers. Good. Do you feel me touching you? Say 'yes' every time."

"Yes, Yes, Yes, Yes, Yes."

"Good, you haven't any tendon or nerve damage. I'll just inject some local anaesthetic and then stitch you up."

It didn't take long. A suture round a cut artery stopped the bleeding and with half a dozen stitches I closed the wound. "There now it's all over – you're as good as new."

"Huh, I wish you could mend me as easily," Hazel muttered.

"Have we a bed, Sister?" I asked.

"Yes."

"Good, Hazel, we are going to keep you in overnight. You've lost a lot of blood and the rest will do you good. In any case you and I need to have a chat. I'll come back after evening surgery and we'll talk then."

"Thanks, Doctor." She smiled weakly and a pathetic frown creased her forehead.

I found Bill pacing up and down in the empty waiting room. "Hazel's fine," I said, "I've stitched her up and we'll keep her in overnight."

"Did she say anything, Doctor?"

"No nothing – should she?"

"No, no. I just wondered. You don't think I could take her home now?"

"No. She's too upset. I'm coming up after surgery to see her again."

Bill looked uneasy. "Can I see her now?"

"Of course, just go in. I must fly. Bye."

"Bye, thanks, Doc."

When I returned in the evening to see Hazel I found Bill with her. He was sitting on the bed holding her hand.

"Well we seem a lot better, don't we?" I said, smiling at Hazel.

Why doctors address their patients as 'we' I have never discovered. Maybe it's a way of saying you and I are in this together, a sort of 'team talk'.

Hazel smiled. "Thanks, Doctor, I'm fine."

"Good, Bill would you mind leaving us for a blether. I want to talk to Hazel."

"Must I?" he said, somewhat defensively I thought.

"Go on, Bill. You heard what the doctor said," replied Hazel.

Bill reluctantly got up and left. "I'll be in the waiting room if you need me."

"Well Hazel," I said pulling up a chair beside her bed. "What's all the trouble?"

"It's not me, Doctor, it's Bill. I don't think he loves me any more."

"What makes you say that?"

"He's having an affair."

"Are you sure?"

"Oh, I'm sure. I've seen them at it." She blew her nose.

"How long has it being going on?" I asked.

"I don't know, probably several months. A young girl, Julie, was taken on by the estate to help with the

134

pheasants. She's on some youth training scheme. Bill's been keeping funny hours lately; when I ask him why he always blames the extra work with the incubating and rearing of the poults. Well today he forgot his lunchbox. It was a lovely day, so I took it up to the rearing pens. When I got there, there was nobody about and I was about to turn and go away when I heard sounds coming from the grain store. I looked through the window and there they were, hard at it. I nearly fainted. I was violently sick. They heard me and Bill came out. When he saw me he looked absolutely shattered. He went quite white. He was speechless. I turned and ran, jumped into his Land Rover, fortunately the keys were in it, and I drove home."

"Then what?"

"Well I didn't know what to do. I couldn't face life without him. He's the only one I've ever known who understands me. If I couldn't have him I didn't think I could live without him, so I took his cut-throat and... well you know the rest. It was to be our fifth anniversary next week. Aren't men bastards, Doctor."

It wasn't a question. I didn't answer. After a moment I said, "Hazel, do you mind if I speak to Bill? He'll know you've told me all this."

"I don't mind. He says it was a one off and he'll never do it again. But they all say that, don't they? I'll never trust him again, never."

I rang the bell and a nurse appeared.

"Nurse, will you get Hazel a cup of tea, please, whilst I have a word with her husband. I'll be back soon, Hazel," I said as I followed the nurse out of the room. "Nurse," I said under my breath. "Keep an eye on her, we can't take any chances. I don't want her trying to do something stupid again. Stay with her."

Bill was reading a newspaper which he promptly threw down onto another seat.

"Well, Doctor, how is she?"

"Let's go somewhere else and talk." I led him through into an adjacent interview room.

Now I know it's not done nowadays, but I was brought up in a world of rules, boundaries and limits – the bedroom slipper, or the gym shoe and a cuff across the ear. Parents weren't pursued by social workers if wee Johnny was found to have a bruise on his bottom. Life followed a pattern, a set of rules governed behaviour, a stability followed. So when Bill asked me how Hazel was I told him, and told him in the old fashioned straight from the shoulder way, no messing about. "Well, physically she's fine but mentally she's what young people call an 'unhappy bunny' I call it shattered. She'll probably get over it but at the moment she is devastated by your unfaithfulness. She feels she can't ever trust you again." Bill started to speak. I held up my hand.

"Let me finish. Hazel is an insecure girl. I suspect she always has been but she had found happiness and security with you and yet within five years of marriage…"

"No," again Bill tried to interrupt.

"You can have your turn in a minute – as I was saying within five years of marriage, you're having a fling with a girl, a girl just out of school. Have you no self-discipline? Have you no sense of honour and decency? How would you feel if Hazel did the same? Well?" I stopped. I'd probably said too much, but hells bells surely somebody had to tell him. And who else was there?

"Are you finished, Doctor, are you quite done?" Bill was angry. "Well let me just tell you a thing or two. Yes, I was wrong, and I haven't done it before and yes, I suppose I might do it again, but let me tell you why." This time it was he who held up his hand. "You might like to know Hazel and I aren't married."

"What do you mean?" I interrupted in astonishment.

"Just what I said, Hazel and I aren't married. She won't marry me. I've pleaded and pleaded but she refused."

"But your health cards – Mr and Mrs Watson?"

"No. Hazel Watson and William Watson, these are our names. We both had the same surname by birth, but we aren't married. Check her notes, you'll see. Oh I know I was wrong to do what I did but things just blew up. I had planned a weekend away to celebrate our fifth so-called anniversary and had booked in at Gretna

Green, and Hazel had finally agreed to marry me. We were packing last night when she said, 'I can't go through with this. Let's go on as we are. I'm happy, I don't want to get married.'

"I tell you, Doctor, I was cross, bloody furious to be honest. I nearly hit her but I didn't. I stormed out of the house and went down to the pub. She was asleep when I got back and I dozed down on the sofa. We didn't speak at breakfast and I left in a huff. I didn't intend to have a fling with Julie, though god knows she's been trying to lead me on for weeks. This time I said to myself, 'Okay to hell with it, why not?' It was a sort of revenge, okay thoughtless, maybe as you said I've no sense of honour, no decency – but I think you're wrong. And wrong to say what you did. I'm a decent guy. I do know what is right and wrong, and most of all I do love Hazel and I wish I hadn't done it."

He turned his back on me and stood looking out of the window. He placed his head in his hands and leant against the frame. His shoulders began to shake. To see a man, a grown man, cry is one of the most heart-wrenching things I know. It was too late to say I'm sorry, but I did.

"I'm sorry, Bill, I did say too much and said it badly. I do understand. I'm going to have another word with Hazel, come through when you're ready."

I left Bill and walked slowly through to Hazel. I was cross. How many times had she deliberately misled me, and why? Why hadn't she said from the beginning that they were just partners? The state that was fast replacing marriage and proving to be even more unreliable. No more 'my husband' or 'my wife'. Now it was just 'a partner, a friend, an item'. No stability, no discipline, that's what's wrong with the world.

Hazel and the nurse were chatting as I opened the door.

"Thank you, Nurse." She got up and left. "Well Hazel, I've had a chat with Bill."

She looked at me, a questioning frown on her face but no smile. I said nothing but held her stare. She knew he'd told me.

"He told you, didn't he?"

"Yes, but why, Hazel, why didn't you tell me? You deliberately misled me from the beginning."

"I know I'm sorry, really sorry. You see I wanted to get married. I know I was wrong not to tell you, but I felt guilty at not marrying Bill and that's why I didn't tell you. I've wanted to marry him from the beginning, but I couldn't."

"Why not, what on earth stopped you?"

"My mother."

"Your mother?" I said in surprise.

"Yes, my mother. You see my father died when I was seven. He was a ghillie and he fell whilst salmon fishing on the Helmsdale. He fractured his skull on a rock. He was rushed to the hospital in Inverness but never regained consciousness and died within a week. I was all Mother had, I had no brothers or sisters. She was a wonderful mother. She got a job in a hotel in Lairg. They were very good to her and gave her a small flat above one of the garages. She worked so hard. Everything she did, she did for me. Sorry, Doctor, I'm going on a bit but I've never before been able to talk to anyone like this."

"No, no that's all right go on. I'm in no hurry."

She was like a choked drain that had suddenly been unblocked. It all came pouring out, the good, the bad, the lot, clearing itself, running free for the first time in ages.

"I took up the fiddle, highland dancing, Mum was even happy when I took up fishing. You'll be nearer Dad she would say. The trouble started when I began to want to go to dances. I thought at the time she was worried I would do something silly. She was always saying, 'Now be careful, Hazel, and I'm not talking about crossing the road.' I knew what she meant but that was as near to sex education as I ever got from Mum. Looking back on it now I realise she wasn't really worried about me misbehaving; she was worried I would meet someone and fall in love. The irony of it was that if Mum hadn't been such a good mum and helped me so much I would probably never have done so well at school. As a result I got five As and one B in my Highers and went to Edinburgh University. I thought she would be so proud of me, but if she was she didn't show it. She became irritable and was always nagging – it wasn't like her at all. I didn't enjoy university. I missed

Mum, I missed Lairg, I was constantly homesick. Eventually I packed it in and went home. She stopped nagging and was back to her old self. Then I met Bill and slowly it all started up again. 'Where are you going? When will you be in?' On and on, she never gave up.

"Eventually Bill asked me to marry him. I wanted to, but I knew Mum would be upset."

"Let me speak to Mum first," I said.

"'You're too young,' she said, 'besides he's a sailor and you know what sailors are like, here today and gone tomorrow and goodness knows what they get up to when they're away.' Finally she agreed to an engagement, but as time dragged on Bill became more and more impatient and to be honest so did I. In the end she agreed that I could go away and set up house with Bill at Rosyth. Funnily enough Mum seemed to accept that arrangement better than I expected. I suppose she felt as we weren't married I still belonged to her.

"Bill and I were very happy and we tried to go home every month, well I did, Bill couldn't always make it. He was very good to her and I honestly believe she liked him. After Bill left the navy we came here and you know the rest. What on earth are we going to do now? What would you advise, Doctor?"

I smiled. "Hazel, I've spent my life giving advice – my children say I'm the world's expert at giving advice. The trouble is a lot of it is wrong. It's probably easier to find a piece of white heather on a Highland hillside than pick out my good pieces of advice."

"But you must have some idea, Doctor. Honestly what would you do?"

"If you love him, marry him. If you don't, leave him."

"But how do I know if I love him?"

"Can you stand living the rest of your life without him?"

She looked up at me, her frown now gone. "Thank you, Doctor, I think I know what I'll do. Don't worry about me. I'll never do anything stupid again – well not like that anyway."

"I know." I squeezed her hand and left. I went to the waiting room but Bill was gone.

The next morning I went back up to the hospital. "How's Hazel, Sister?"

"She's gone, Doctor. She signed herself out an hour ago we couldn't hold her. I phoned your house, but you'd gone. Her husband collected her."

"Did he say anything?"

"No, well not apart from thanking us for looking after his wife."

I went round to their house but it was empty.

About ten days later, I was having breakfast when the post arrived.

"Well I never," said my wife.

"What are you 'nevering' about?" I said, trying to concentrate on a difficult Sudoku.

"A postcard for you from the Smithy at Gretna Green."

"Gretna Green, I don't know anyone there."

"Oh I think you do."

I took the postcard, turned it over and read it. *Many thanks. Lots of love Mr & Mrs Watson. P.S. Mum was a witness!*

It's not what you know, it's who you know.

One of the advantages of practising medicine in the same practice and not flitting about to other places is that you not only get to know your patients, but you also build up a valuable relationship with your local hospital consultant colleagues. This is well illustrated in the following short tale. I was invited by a Doctor Wilson to do a locum in yet another Highland village. I readily accepted the invitation as I always enjoyed working in these somewhat remote areas. It was to prove a fairly easy week. The list size was only about one thousand and the patients were, he told me, 'pretty self-sufficient', and he didn't think I would be very busy. On the Friday at the end of my week's locum, which I may say was, as he had suggested, very quiet, I received a phone call from Doctor Wilson; his wife had fallen down and broken her hip. It was to be pinned the following day in St Thomas' Hospital in London where they were holidaying and he saw no chance of returning with her for at least another week. Could I possibly help and stay on? As I had nothing else to do I was happy to say yes.

Another quiet week and no likelihood of being disturbed at night and another cheque: it seemed a real sinecure. After enjoying another quiet Friday and not being called out of bed between eleven p.m. and three a.m., which I may say was the norm in my previous practice in the Borders, I decided to go to the local Highland Games on the Saturday. I had my mobile phone and I checked that reception for it was good at the Games field. Taking my own deckchair and an appropriate picnic lunch I settled down for the afternoon's entertainment. Tossing the caber, I find exhausting even just to watch but I have to say the participants that day were remarkable skilful. Apart from their strength, their accuracy was remarkable (the caber is about nineteen feet and six inches long and weighs a hundred and seventy-five pounds!). The contestants that afternoon came from as far afield as Australia, New Zealand and Canada – and of course from England and Scotland. I think that several of the contestants travel round the Highlands competing each week at a different Games for the prize money that the events attract.

As the day wore on I was further entertained by the various other field events, the cycle races, and finally the track events. I would have waited for the final of the half mile, and the relay races, but as so often happens in the Highlands around five p.m. my tranquillity was destroyed by the advent of the midges. It doesn't seem to matter what you do, they devour you. I was reminded of a BBC programme on the Helmsdale River. An attractive young lass was interviewing an elderly ghillie who had fished the river for over fifty years. She asked him, "What's your abiding memory of the Helmsdale River?"

"Midges," he replied.

"Midges?" she said slightly puzzled.

"Aye, you kill one and a million come to the funeral."

Anyway, I was not waiting for the funeral, so I rose from my chair, folded it up, and left in a haste for the security of my car.

The rest of the weekend was unbelievably quiet. An acute middle ear infection in a three-year-old and a twenty-one-year-old with a sprained ankle caused by falling whilst competing in a race up and down Ben Bhraggie was all I had to deal with.

On the evening of the Monday of the second week I was late going to bed; my wife had gone up at ten p.m. but I was keen to see the end of my favourite film: *The Best Years of Their Lives* and it was close on eleven when I finally went to bed. I started to read but couldn't and fell fast asleep. I was woken by the telephone.

"Hello, Doctor Neville speaking."

"Ah Doctor, sorry to disturb you, a patient of yours has requested a visit."

"Who's speaking?"

"Oh so sorry, it's Constable Sutherland from the police station."

"What's the problem, Officer, it's almost one o'clock?"

146

"Oh I don't know, he just said he needed a doctor."

"Who is it anyway?" I asked, now wide awake.

"A Mr Taylor and I don't know what's wrong with the gentleman, he just says he wants you."

"Well I need to know a bit more about what the problem is.," I replied, anxious not to have to get out of bed.

"Are you saying you won't go, Doctor?" The constable was obviously becoming a bit annoyed.

"No, I'm just trying to find out if it is necessary to go now or can it wait till the morning?"

"I don't know, I'm not the doctor. Will you go?"

"Yes, I suppose I have to, what's his address?"

"It's the caravan park. Site twenty-four. Goodnight, Doctor."

With a heavy sigh I rose, dressed and set off to see Mr Taylor.

As it turned out there was only one caravan in the park and a pretty miserable one it was too: rusty wheels, grey stained body work and a satellite aerial bent almost double hanging from a window, all very uninviting. I knocked on the door.

"Come in."

I opened the door and climbed up into the caravan; the inside was worse than the outside. A poor gaslight was not the reason for me tripping in the narrow passage; it was an empty beer can, as it turned out one of many. "Mr Taylor?" I asked, holding out my hand.

"Yes, who are you?" replied an overweight man ignoring my outstretched hand. He was holding a glass in one hand and a beer can in the other. "Will you have a beer?" he asked.

"No, thank you," I replied. "I'm the doctor you sent for."

"Oh yes, are you sure you don't want a beer?"

"Look it's nearly two o'clock in the morning and I didn't come all this way to drink beer. What is it you want?"

"I feel terrible, Doctor. You'll need to do something for me; I can't eat, can't sleep and nobody visits me. I can't think why. still now you are here can you do something?"

"What did you have in mind?" I replied, for want of something better to say.

"Well that's your job. Are you sure you won't…?"

"No, and I think you shouldn't either," I said as he bent down and picked up another can. I realised this was not going to be easy. There was nothing I could do for him tonight but how was I to get away? I couldn't just up and off.

"I'll tell you what I will do. I'll get your notes from the surgery in the morning and find out about your health history and you come and see me at two o'clock tomorrow afternoon. How does that sound?"

"So you think you will be able to help?" he asked pathetically.

"Definitely," I replied rising from my seat, and before he could reply I wished him goodnight and turned to leave.

"Goodbye, Doctor."

I climbed down from the caravan and drove home. I wondered what his health records would contain.

As it so happened the only note in his file was a brief discharge letter from the district psychiatric hospital dated a week previously; it simply confirmed his discharge and said a letter would follow. It seemed likely that he had only signed on with the practice recently as there were no records through from where he had previously lived.

He didn't come to see me at two o'clock. To be perfectly honest I wasn't disappointed, I really hoped I'd never see him again. Sadly, that was not to be.

Two days later, or rather two nights later I was awoken from my slumbers by the phone.

"Hello, Doctor Neville here."

"Ah Doctor, I'm afraid it's PC Sutherland again."

My heart sank. "Yes, Constable, don't tell me it's Mr Taylor again?"

"Yes, I'm afraid so. He wants you to visit him; apparently you made quite a hit the last time."

"Officer, it was a complete waste of time then, he was just drunk, and I'm sure it will be the same this time. I offered him an appointment at my surgery, but he failed to turn up. I don't see why I should turn out at one in the morning again to see him."

"So, you won't go?"

"Well give me one good reason why I should and don't tell me it's because he wants me," I said feeling my temper rising.

"I thought you would be reluctant to go, just like last time, so I sent a police cadet to check if it was really necessary." The constable sounded triumphant.

"Huh, and what did the police cadet have to say?" I asked a trifle sarcastically."

"He said the man appeared very ill and was lying on the floor, mumbling. He reckoned the man had had a stroke."

I realised I could not safely refuse to go. "I suppose I'd better go then, goodnight," and I put the phone down. Half an hour later, now ten to three, I arrived at the caravan. I opened the door and walked in. The cadet was right, Mr Taylor was lying on the floor but that was all he was right about.

"Doctor," Mr Taylor said as I entered, "are you going to join me with a beer this time?" He looked up with a smile and a glass in one hand and a can in the other.

"No, I didn't come here to drink. Why the hell didn't you come to my surgery at two o'clock as I requested?"

"I couldn't because when I woke up it was after two and I don't believe in keeping doctors waiting and I knew you would be cross."

"So instead you pull me out of bed in the middle of the night."

"The policeman who came to see me said I needed a doctor," Taylor said this with a triumphant self-satisfied smirk.

"Right that does it; I shall send an ambulance for you in the morning."

"Where do you want me to go?"

"Don't tempt me," I muttered under my breath. "I am sending you back to the psychiatric hospital you were in two weeks ago."

"Okay, if you think that's for the best but let's part friends, have a beer before you go."

"No, thank you, I am going back to bed. Goodnight." I turned round and exited the caravan and went home hoping never to see Mr Taylor again.

In the morning I phoned the psychiatric hospital. "May I speak to the waiting psychiatric houseman please?"

"One moment please, I'll get her for you."

A moment later a rather brusque young lady came on the line. "Who's speaking?"

"It's Doctor Neville, I am doing a locum for Doctor Wilson and I have a patient I would like you to admit."

"We've no beds at the moment; who is it anyway?"

"A Mr Sutherland and—"

She rudely interrupted me, "Not that awful man who lives in a caravan?"

"Yes, I'm afraid it is."

"No, I haven't a bed for him; he's just a drunk."

"That's as maybe," I replied, realising I had a battle on my hands with this particular houseman, "but you haven't heard what I have to say about why I want him admitted."

"I don't think I need to; I have had enough of that man to last a lifetime."

"Right put me through to your consultant and we will see what she or he has to say. It's obvious that you and I are not going to agree."

"Very well but she, Doctor Walker, will agree with me. Hold on." I waited a few minutes and then I heard the phone being lifted.

"Hello Doctor, Helen Walker here, who am I speaking to?"

"Good morning Doctor Walker, it's Doctor Peter Neville."

"Who?" she said with a rather surprised tone in her voice.

"Doctor Peter Neville, you won't know me, I'm doing a locum for Doctor Wilson."

"Not Doctor Neville from Hawick? I don't believe it!"

"Yes, you've got it in one."

"How lovely to talk to you after such a long time, you'll remember me; well I was Helen Burns then and just a registrar, but since then I have married and became a consultant here."

"Of course I remember you," I replied. To be honest I hadn't a clue who she was and neither of her names reminded me. "Congratulations on both counts; you must be very pleased."

"Absolutely, it's a great place to work and most of my patients are just like yours used to be. I did enjoy our meetings every last Monday in the month in your surgery to discuss our mutual problem patients."

"Yes, they were fun, weren't they?" (I did remember the meetings; we thought they were a waste of time but obviously they can't have been!)

"Well, Peter, what can I do for you, nothing too complicated I hope?"

"To be honest it's a bit of a favour I'm asking."

"Fire away."

"Well you know Sandy Taylor?"

"What, not that drunk?"

"I'm afraid it is."

"Has he been bothering you? We can soon put a stop to that."

"I hope so... Helen." For a moment I had forgotten her first name. "He has had me to his caravan at two in the morning on both Monday and Wednesday of this week."

"I'm surprised you went."

"Well I wouldn't have done if the police hadn't made it difficult for me to say no. I did try to persuade him to come to the surgery, but he never came. Do you think you can help? Your houseman said there were no beds and 'they' didn't want Taylor back?"

"Of course I can help. How long are you planning to be up here for?"

"Probably another ten days."

"No problem, we will keep him in for a fortnight and to make sure you've gone home I will ring the surgery to make sure Doctor Wilson is back from his holiday before I discharge him."

"Helen you are a treasure. Next time I'm up here, you and I must meet up for a gossip. How many years is it anyway?"

"At least ten," she replied. "I came here in '86."

"In that case you had better wear a carnation in your hair or I might not recognise you."

She laughed. Little did she know I was serious.

Sandy Taylor was admitted that afternoon and I wasn't out of bed again. So I think I'm right when I say sometimes it is 'not what you know, but who you know'– don't you agree?

Too good to be true

Doctor Jeremy Fortescue Hastings was a carefree dashing charmer; the patients loved him, the children loved him and the nurses loved him. Oh yes, the nurses loved him. He was the medical profession's answer to James Bond and Errol Flynn rolled into one. Six feet three inches tall, fourteen stone, curly black hair always immaculately groomed but with that contrived disorder suggesting he had just run his fingers through it, or more likely someone else had. Clean shaven, with a wide welcoming, almost suggestive, smile and glistening white regular teeth that would have been the envy of any orthodontist.

Doctor Hastings had applied for a vacancy that had arisen in the practice as the result of the sudden death of my senior partner on the steps of the maternity hospital as he was leaving after having carried out a difficult delivery of twins.

I had tried for six months to run the practice by myself, and although I enjoyed the significant rise in my income, the endless on-call work became too much for me.

"If you don't take on a partner you'll end up like Doctor Stewart," my wife would say, and I knew she was right. So I placed an advertisement in the *British Medical Journal* for 'an Assistant with a View' – this would give me the chance to see how good the applicant was and, if he was good, I would make him a partner at the end of the year. (These were the days when almost all GPs were men.) There were over thirty applicants for the job and eventually by careful selection I cut them down to three. I excluded anyone who was over thirty-five, who was unmarried (after all, who would answer his phone if he was called out? Me!) and sadly any females. The idea of having a pretty young female, whilst all right in theory, was no good in practice. Who would do the work when she got married or had babies? Again, me! Anyway, there I was with a short list of three. The two I didn't take were both Aberdeen graduates, both had good CVs. One was an earnest young man, bespectacled and a trifle untidy, and very interested in what time off he would be given and how many weeks holidays he would have each year; the other was more laid back, possibly even a bit casual, and expressed considerable interest in how much money he could make. Neither had a hope of competing with Jeremy Fortescue Hastings. As you might expect, Jeremy had a gorgeous wife.

"We've no children yet," he said. "Sally's been too busy. You may have seen her on the box. She was in a recent episode of *Men Behaving Badly*."

She was tall, slender and, inevitably, blonde. She had tantalising blue eyes that invited trouble. I wondered who had chased who. Maybe they both had their hands full. How right I was, but we'll come to that.

Sally and Jeremy came round for dinner shortly after they arrived. I also invited the Rev. Charles Green and his wife Penny to join us. Sally looked stunning. She wore a tight-fitting buttercup yellow dress and very high heels. My wife thought the dress too short. I didn't and nor did Charles, who appeared totally mesmerised by her. She sat between us at dinner and had it not been for the charm that oozed from Jeremy and entranced our wives, Charles and I would most certainly have been in hot water from our wives for paying such close attention to Sally. After coffee Jeremy said they must be off as he didn't like being late midweek. I nodded approvingly. Charles and I stood up. Sally shook hands with Charles and Penny then turned to me. "Thank you, Peter, a delightful evening." And leaning forward she kissed me softly on the cheek. I smiled at Charles, one up to me.

Jeremy then kissed my wife. "Wonderful evening, best soufflé I think I've ever tasted."

"Well, Charles, what do you think of my new acquisition?" I asked as we settled back in our chairs with a glass of vintage port. However it was Penny who answered.

"I thought she was gorgeous but too beautiful to be good."

"You can't say that," replied her husband. "After all, remember what the Lord said in St John's Gospel chapter—"

"Oh, leave that till Sunday, dear, you know what I mean; she's trouble, don't you agree, June?"

"You may well be right, Penny. I think Jeremy's got his hands full, such a nice young man."

"Yes I agree," Penny replied, "such nice manners, so rare nowadays."

I sipped my port and smiled. Yes, a charming couple or a volcano waiting to erupt.

Three months passed before I noticed the first warning rumbles. It was after evening surgery. I was on alone as it was Jeremy's half day. I went up to the cottage hospital to see an elderly lady who I had admitted earlier in the day with chest pain. I was surprised to see Jeremy's BMW coupé parked in the hospital car park – a real tart-trap my unmarried but attractive secretary called it – rather enviously I thought. What on earth was he doing at the hospital? I wondered. The hospital is a single-storey building with six single rooms, and at the far end two eight-bedded wards and the operating theatre. The theatre was rarely used nowadays, and hadn't been for several years, as all operations were now done at the district hospital twenty miles away. As I walked down the corridor, through the swing doors of the theatre suite hurried a pretty young staff nurse. When she saw me she stopped, half turned as if to go back, changed her mind and carried on. As she passed me I said, "Good evening, Nurse Ramsay."

She nodded, muttered something inaudible, blushed and hurried past me. I looked back at her and was surprised to see that her uniform was unbuttoned down her back. As I turned into the ward the theatre doors opened again and out strolled Jeremy.

"Hello, Jeremy," I said. "I thought you were off duty."

"Oh I am, just popped up to collect some bandages. I am giving a talk to the young mothers' group tomorrow on first aid." Funny I thought, he wasn't carrying any bandages. On my way out, I dropped into the nurses' duty room to write up some sedation for my patient. Nurse Ramsay was sitting behind her desk, her back to me, her buttons still undone. She looked up.

"Can I help you, Doctor?"

"Not really, I just want to write up a sedative for Mrs Molloy, she seems a bit better. By the way did Doctor Hastings find what he was looking for?"

"Oh, he wasn't looking for anything, he just wanted to see where we used to operate."

She turned back to her desk and, for the second time that evening, blushed.

I smiled to myself. "Goodnight," I replied and went off home. I had little doubt that Jeremy was inspecting more than the operating table.

My suspicion that my new assistant was cheating on Sally was confirmed about six weeks later. I had offered to do duty over the Calcutta Cup weekend so that Jeremy could go to Murrayfield to watch the rugby. He phoned me early on Saturday morning.

"Hello, Peter, no outstanding problems other than Jenny in the maternity home. She's not doing much but it's her third and I think she'll crack on pretty soon. I'm off, see you Monday. Hope you're not too busy. Bye."

"Bye, have a good time."

Good time? I'll bet he did. Half an hour later as I was filling up at the garage a BMW coupé flew past, its roof down, and Jeremy's black curly hair was blowing in the wind as was the blonde hair of his passenger, Nurse Ramsay.

But Nurse Ramsay didn't last long. Soon it was Sister Edwards, a pleasant if slightly erratic woman who, although only in her late thirties, was already twice married and twice divorced. She appeared totally unable to control her hormones. I was surprised Jeremy bothered. Next it was my envious secretary. This was too close to home and I remonstrated with him.

"You can't go on like this. It's not fair on Sally and it's bad for the practice."

He smiled. "You're just jealous, Peter, and Sally's away a lot, besides I've got to keep the engine running – awful if it stalled," and slapping me across the shoulders he strolled off whistling. I didn't see much of Sally, but June had her round for tea a couple of times and remarked how well she was looking.

"She's taken up fishing, apparently loves it," my wife said.

"Good for her. They say women make better fishers than men," I replied.

"Yes they probably do," agreed my wife, "more patient, gentler touch, something to do with their vermins."

"Maybe, but I think you mean pheromones. Jeremy has probably encouraged her; he's quite a fanatic when it comes to fishing."

"You're quite right he did. Apparently he arranged for Paul Harker, who often ghillies for him, to take her in hand."

Paul was a nice lad. He worked as a laboratory technician at the district hospital and lived with his wife and two small children in one of the hospital cottages just inside the main gates. His father had been a full-time ghillie and Paul had inherited his father's keenness and skill. His wife had a part-time job as a radiographer and occasionally did holiday relief at the cottage hospital though most of the time worked in the district hospital. She had a refreshingly cheerful manner and was always smiling and friendly – too friendly as I was to discover. Paul thought nothing of motoring the twenty odd miles to join Jeremy for some evening fishing, and when the sea trout were running the pair of them would be on the river till the early hours. I bumped into Paul one evening just as I was closing up the surgery. He was wearing his Harris Tweed plus twos and a thick-ribbed polo neck jersey. He touched the brim of his deerstalker which was covered with all manner of flies, all sizes and all colours.

"Off fishing?" I asked.

"No, actually I promised to hand in Jeremy's stethoscope. I found it on the floor of my car. It must have fallen out of his pocket last night when we were fishing."

"That was kind of you, but you shouldn't have bothered.

Jeremy left at five this morning for Cape Wrath. He's keen to have a go on the limestone lochs, he says they're supposed to be very good. But you'll know all about that. Thanks anyway."

"Oh it's no trouble; I was coming over anyway to give Sally a lesson in Spey casting."

"How's she coming on? I could never master it, and after embedding an Aly Shrimp in my right ear in a high wind went back to overhead."

"Yes, you have to be careful in a wind. Sometimes you need to do a double Spey."

"Good god, if I can't do a single, I certainly can't do a double." He laughed.

"Well must be off, see you," and touching the brim of his multicoloured deerstalker he climbed into his battered Suzuki.

Things came to a head about two weeks later. I had just seen my last patient and was writing up some notes when Jeremy popped his head round my door.

"Can you swap duty and do tonight and I'll do Friday, Peter? The sea trout are running and I don't want to miss them."

"No problem. Take care the river's up a bit after all the rain. Are you taking Paul with you?"

"No. Oh didn't I tell you. Poor chap was admitted to hospital last night with an acute appendix."

"I'm sorry to hear that. Well you be careful on your own." I worried a bit about his night-time fishing. He and Paul would think nothing of staying on the river till two or three in the morning.

About midnight the phone rang. It was the mother of one of my unstable young asthmatics. "Please come quick, Doctor, Angie's bad."

"I'll come right away."

Angie was bad. She lay propped up in bed leaning forward with her arms across the bed table, her shoulders hunched, struggling for breath. Her hair, wet with sweat, straggled down both sides of her agonised face. She looked imploringly at me but didn't speak. She couldn't. I gave her some intravenous steroid, started her nebuliser and phoned the ambulance.

"Will she be all right?"

"Yes, Mrs Williams, Angie will be fine. I'll go with her in the ambulance. You follow in your car with her things like we did the last time. Remember?"

"Yes."

I phoned for the ambulance and by the time it arrived, Angie was beginning to improve but for safety's sake I travelled with her. As we entered the gates of the hospital we passed Paul's house and parked outside was Jeremy's BMW coupé. So much for the running sea trout! I decided I really must have it out with him, but as Sally and he had invited us to a supper party the following evening I would have to wait. I passed Angie over to the waiting physician and the ambulance ran me home.

The following morning Jeremy came in whistling as usual.

"Well how did the fishing go?" I asked.

"Fine, landed two three pounders – we'll have them tonight for supper."

He really was incorrigible.

I was last getting away from the surgery that evening and the party was in full swing when we arrived. Sally was standing silhouetted in the bow window. She was wearing an off the shoulder black three-quarter length dress which was high enough to be interesting but low enough to be decent. A gold choker round her neck glistened in the setting sun.

"Hello, Peter," she said, and we kissed on both cheeks. "I was just saying to David what a fabulous view we have, don't you agree?"

David, our local vet, nodded but I reckoned the view he was referring to was Sally. There was no doubt the view was outstanding. From the window stretching as far as you could see was a heather and bracken moor climbing steadily to the rounded peak of Ben Var. A herd of deer numbering about twenty had started down the side of the hill heading for the waters of Loch Lundy.

"It's fabulous," I said. "It's God's country."

"Yes, it is God's country," said a voice in my ear.

"Evening, Charles," I said, turning to greet the minister. He squeezed between David and me and kissed Sally good evening.

"My brother can't stand the view," said Sally. He prefers New York, can you believe it. Last time he was here on an evening like this, the sun was just setting behind Ben Var and the heather looked as if it was on fire and do you know what he said?"

"No, tell us," said David staring adoringly at Sally.

"He said, 'It's ghastly there's just miles and miles of bugger all.' I think he'd prefer a tenement block to the Taj Mahal." We all laughed. "Well come on, supper's ready, let's go in. Jeremy sit everybody down and I'll just be a minute."

Sally came back holding aloft a large Lochinver pottery dish on which lay two gleaming silver sea trout. "Look what Jeremy caught last night. Isn't he a clever boy? Took you quite a while, didn't it, darling?" Jeremy had the grace to look slightly uncomfortable; not a bad alibi, I thought.

"Oh not too long," he said, slightly shamefacedly I thought.

"Well I think you're marvellous, the way you fish till two and still manage to get up in time for morning surgery. Don't you, Peter?" Sally turned to me for approval.

"Absolutely," I muttered. Well what else could I say? You had to admire Jeremy's alibi. I couldn't help feeling sorry for Sally, tied to a rogue like Jeremy and yet I never heard her complain.

About a month after the party Jeremy went away on a refresher course. Two days later Sally phoned me.

"Peter, sorry to bother you, I slipped in the bath last night and I think I've cracked a rib. Can I pop in and see you?"

"Certainly not, my dear, I'll look in after the surgery."

"Are you sure it's no trouble?"

"No trouble at all. You stay in bed and I'll be round about eleven."

"Thank you so much. Just come straight up."

The last patient at my morning surgery was Paul. "Well how goes it?"

"Fine thanks. Can I go back to work on Monday?"

"Yes, I don't see why not. Avoid lifting heavy weights and leave off the fishing for another week or two."

"Thanks, Doctor." Paul stood up and looked around.

"Something bothering you, Paul?"

"No, just habit I suppose. I lost my deerstalker yesterday and I feel underdressed without it and keep looking for it."

"Well it's not here or I'd have seen it. You couldn't miss it, could you? Ask at the reception desk on your way out."

"Bye, Doctor, thanks."

"Bye."

I declined my usual cup of coffee after the surgery had finished and hurried off to see Sally. She was sitting up in bed supported by four pillows. Her blonde hair cascaded carelessly down over her shoulders. A touch of pale pink lipstick and a suggestion of Chanel No 5 combined with an almost, but not quite, transparent nightie was enough to bring any reasonable man to his knees.

"Well now, let's have a look." I don't know if she noticed my trembling hands or thumping heart; she just sat there smiling sweetly. The old adage 'you can make a patient of your mistress, but you mustn't make a mistress of your patient' flashed across my brain. I took a deep breath. "Well let's have a listen." I took my stethoscope out and sounded Sally's chest.

"Well, Peter, what do you think?"

I gave a nervous cough. "I think you're right; you do have a cracked rib but no lung damage. Just take life quietly for a week or ten days and you should be fine. I'll pop in again in a couple of days. By the way how's the fishing going?"

"Oh I haven't done any for a bit. Paul's been ill and I haven't seen him for a month."

"He's starting work again next week."

"Oh good, then I expect he'll be in touch." She blushed slightly or was it a trick of the light glinting through the Venetian blinds.

"Oh well, see you Thursday." I made my way downstairs.

Her voice followed me.

"Please shut the front door on your way out."

"Okay."

The coat and hat rack stood behind the open door. I took my coat off the peg, threw it over my arm, and pulled the door shut – well that's what I meant to do but it was jammed on something. A piece of rug had got caught under it. I knelt down and slid my hand behind the door to try to pull the rug out. Eventually it came away, but it wasn't a rug, it was a deerstalker covered with all manner of flies. There was only one like it – and it wasn't Jeremy's. Ah well, I thought, what's sauce for the goose is sauce for the gander. I decided that under the circumstances I would take my old gardener's advice: 'When in doubt say nowt.' It was good advice.

One Sunday morning in early September I was sitting enjoying a leisurely breakfast and trying to solve a fiendish Sudoku in *The Sunday Times*, when my wife, who was thumbing through her diary, broke the silence.

"When does Jeremy become a partner?"

"What?" I said, only half hearing the question.

"When is Jeremy becoming a partner? He will have been here a year at the end of next month."

"Gosh that's right, how time flies. Well actually I haven't decided."

"What do you mean you haven't decided?"

"Well to be perfectly frank, I haven't decided whether to take him on as a partner or not."

"Oh darling, he's a great success. He's very charming, good looking, perfect manners, and everybody loves him – and he's a good fisherman."

"Yes, but his fishing skill is hardly relevant."

"But he's a good doctor, isn't he?"

"Yes."

"Well what's the problem?"

I hadn't told my wife about Nurse Ramsay and the others, so I wasn't surprised at her enthusiasm for me to appoint Jeremy. Before I could answer her question, the phone rang.

"I'll take it," I said, relieved that it had interrupted our conversation. "Hello, Doctor Neville here."

"Hi Peter, it's me, I'm in a spot of bother at the maternity home. Mrs Watson has been pushing for about an hour and she's not making much progress and the foetal heart rate is beginning to worry me."

"I'll come at once," I replied. "Darling, I'm off to the mat home, Jeremy is worried about Helen Watson."

"Oh no, I hope she'll be all right."

"I'm off." I picked up my bag and hurried out to my car. My wife and I both knew Helen well. She had been our daily help for years until out of the blue, at the age of forty-six, she married our postie and surprised us even

169

more when the following year she announced she was going to have a baby. I asked Jeremy to look after her as I felt she was almost one of the family and it would be better if I didn't. Now I know that all babies are precious but this one was even more important because at her age the chances of her having another were very low. I drove down quickly, parked beside Jeremy's BMW and hurried into the home.

"Thanks for coming, Peter," said Jeremy.

"Hello, Helen," I said, placing a hand on her forehead. "How's it going?"

"Hello, Doctor, good to see you, I don't seem to be very good at this. Oh here's another pain coming."

"Come on, Helen, you're doing fine – *push!*" said Sister Scott, who had seen it all so many times before. I watched Helen as she went blue in the face, pushing as hard as she could, her hands grasping the sides of the bed, her knuckles clenched and white.

"Jeremy, would you like me to examine, Helen?"

"Yes please."

I scrubbed up quickly. "Helen, I'm just going to examine you to see how baby's doing."

"Push," said Sister.

"I can see the wee one's head, Helen, it won't be long now." I turned to Jeremy. "You'll need forceps."

"Yes, will you do it?" adding under his breath, "I've never done a forceps delivery?"

"No, no, it's time you did; you know how to, don't you?"

Turning to Helen, he said, "Helen, I'm going to freeze your bottom and we will deliver the baby with forceps. Everything is going to be fine, all you have to do is push when I tell you to and we'll have your baby out in a few minutes."

I wiped Helen's face with a moist face cloth. "You'll be fine now, just one or two more pushes."

"One more push, Helen, well done, it's coming. Well done here's your baby son," and Jeremy held him up for Helen to see. He took one look at his mother and let out a lusty cry. I have never been able to relax at a delivery until I hear that first cry.

I didn't realise how tense I was until Helen turned to me and said, "Doctor, could you please not grip my hand so tight," and burst into tears. "Oh thank you, Doctor Hastings, you are wonderful – what would I have done without you? And you, Sister, but I don't think I'll have any more."

Sister smiled: she had heard that so many times. She blew her nose and I do believe I saw a tear in her eye. She always kept her emotions under control, but I knew better than most that, although she maintained she would remain single all her life, there had been someone in the past, but that's another story: a secret between her and me.

"I'm off, Helen," I said. "My wife will be so pleased. Bye. Thanks, Sister. Jeremy, pop in for a cup of tea on your way home."

My wife was standing at the front door and as I climbed out of the car she ran forward. "Tell me?"

"It's fine, everything's fine. She has a baby boy and they are both fine."

"Oh darling, I'm so relieved." And she burst into tears as she hugged me.

"Steady on, love."

"I know I'm daft, but I was so worried, weren't you?"

"Oh yes, but men aren't supposed to cry."

"I know. I love you, you know."

I hugged her; weren't we lucky to still be so close after forty years of marriage.

Jeremy dropped in as I suggested and as he drank his tea, we discussed the technical aspects of the delivery. "You know, Peter, I have never seen a case like that before. Of course I've read about it, but it's different when you meet it for the first time in the cold light of day."

"I know, the first time for everything is often difficult: the first time you carry out a difficult procedure, the first time you see someone die, the first time you tell someone they've got cancer. I could go on forever, the problem for us, and I mean us GPs, is that we don't get it right all the time; we can't. We do make mistakes and they can be disastrous. Sometimes the public expect too much – you can't blame them. I think we have to be able to say, 'I'm sorry' and that's not always easy and it's not always enough."

172

My wife interjected, "That's enough of your sermon for a Sunday afternoon, you're getting like Charles."

Jeremy stood up. "I must be going. I'll look in and see Helen and her baby on my way home. Thanks, Peter, I can't tell you how grateful I am, I've learnt a lot today. Bye." And off he went.

"Will we have a party to celebrate Jeremy becoming a partner?" June asked almost before Jeremy was out of earshot.

"No, darling, I'm not taking him on."

"Why on earth not? You must be mad."

"Maybe," I replied. Then I proceeded to tell her all about Jeremy and Sally's rather erratic behaviour. When I had finished, I sat back and waited.

"I see," she said. "Well if it's any comfort for you I agree, but I don't envy you the task of telling him."

"Do you think I should tell them together?"

My wife hesitated. "Yes, but be careful, you don't know if they know about each other's high jinks."

"Let's get it over with. You ring Sally and ask them round for supper."

"When?"

"Tonight."

"What, you mean tonight, isn't that a bit hasty?".

"No, well maybe it is, but let's get it over with. Why not ask them for Friday?"

And so it was that Jeremy and Sally joined us for dinner on Friday. I suspected that Jeremy had an inkling that I would want to talk about a partnership agreement. I had given the matter a lot of thought during the week, and to be honest I didn't know how to tell him without hurting him.

"What will you have, June, the usual?"

"Yes please."

Jeremy stood up from the sofa where he had been sitting with Sally.

"Let me help you, Peter."

"Sally?"

"Something soft please."

"Jeremy?"

"Yes, soft please, I'm on duty."

"Of course. Well I'm not, so I'll have a large G & T." I certainly needed one. "Cheers everyone. Well, Sally, have you enjoyed your stay in the Highlands?"

"Yes, it's been an eye-opener, hasn't it, darling?" Sally replied, squeezing Jeremy's hand and looking deep into his eyes. He smiled and held her gaze; I sensed they were sharing a secret. I looked at my wife and she frowned and nodded her head as if to say, 'Go on, get on with it'. I took a deep breath and cleared my throat.

"Yes, Peter, it's been a most productive year, I've learnt so much, I had no idea I knew so little."

"I'm so glad it's not been a waste of time," I replied, "and that brings me to why we invited you over tonight. I expect you were wondering about the partnership. I'm sorry—" but before I could finish the sentence Jeremy interrupted me.

"No need to be sorry that you haven't mentioned it before. I should have raised the matter with you, but I chickened out, Peter, because I, well Sally and I, didn't want to upset you and June." He smiled briefly at us both. "You see, Peter, Sally and I have decided to leave here."

"But why?" I said, hardly able to believe my ears and trying not to sound relieved.

"We are going to Australia."

"But why?"

"Well to be truthful we would love to have stayed, wouldn't we, Sally?"

She smiled, blew her nose and said, "We certainly would."

"So what's stopping you?" I said in a rash moment, but actually at that moment I actually believed I had changed my mind.

"Well to be absolutely honest, Peter, we've, as I said before, learnt a lot in the last year, not just about medicine but about ourselves. We've both been a bit foolish."

"Or wrong," interrupted Sally.

"Yes, darling, you're right, we've behaved badly at times. It would be wrong to stay here – people would talk. It wouldn't be fair on you. So that's why we are going well away."

"For good?" I asked.

"We don't know yet. We would love to think the answer was no and that one day we would return. I've signed a contract for a year."

And then I said something that took us all, including myself, by surprise.

"I'll not take on another partner, and if at the end of the year you and Sally want to come back here, the partnership is yours."

Sally jumped up, burst into tears and hugged me. Jeremy stood up and with a quiver in his voice said, "Thanks, Peter," and shook me firmly by the hand.

June came with me to the door to see them off. Clutching my right arm she waved, and whispered in my ear, "Well done, darling, you're wonderful, that's what I wanted too. But who will do all the work. You can't do it all by yourself."

"I'll advertise for a locum, preferably a middle-aged spinster ... On second thoughts, how about you applying for the job?" My wife smiled but said nothing and continued waving to the departing car.